HOMELAND
OF
MY BODY

HOMELAND
OF
MY BODY

NEW AND SELECTED POEMS

RICHARD BLANCO

BEACON PRESS
BOSTON

BEACON PRESS
Boston, Massachusetts
www.beacon.org

Beacon Press books
are published under the auspices of
the Unitarian Universalist Association of Congregations.

26 25 24 23   8 7 6 5 4 3 2 1

This book is printed on acid-free paper that meets the uncoated paper
ANSI/NISO specifications for permanence as revised in 1992.

Text design and composition by Kim Arney

Several poems in this volume have been slightly revised from their original
versions in the respective collections where they first appeared.

Library of Congress Cataloging-in-Publication Data
Names: Blanco, Richard, author.
Title: Homeland of my body : new and selected poems / Richard Blanco.
Description: Boston : Beacon Press, 2023. I Summary: "A rich, accomplished,
intensely intimate collection with two full sections of new poems
bookending Blanco's selections from his five previous volumes.
"An engineer, poet, Cuban American . . . his poetry bridges cultures and
languages—a mosaic of our past, our present, and our future-reflecting
a nation that is hectic, colorful, and still becoming." —President Joe
Biden, conferring the National Humanities Medal
on Richard Blanco, 2023" — Provided by publisher.
Identifiers: LCCN 2023025939 I ISBN 978-0-8070-1297-0 (hardcover) I
ISBN 978-0-8070-1298-7 (ebook)
Subjects: LCGFT: Poetry.
Classification: LCC PS3552.L36533 H66 2023 I DDC 811/.54—dc23/
eng/20230605
LC record available at https://lccn.loc.gov/2023025939

For Mark Neveu:

my first friend,
my first & only husband,
my first family,
my first reader,
my first and last
everything.

CONTENTS

FROM DIRECTIONS TO THE BEACH OF THE DEAD

HERE I AM: NEW POEMS PART 2

HOMELAND
OF
MY BODY

RADIANT BEINGS

New Poems
Part 1

THE SPLINTERING

As a boy I was all body, my body part of all
that was. My ears were the wind my cheeks

heard. My mouth the thunder that roared in
my chest. My face in the face of rain puddles

cupped in my palms. My lips the wet petals
my nose kissed. And I blindly saw the stars

as my eyes luring me that night to climb up
our backyard mango tree. Its trunk the will

of my spine, my arms every branch's arms
coddling the wind. Its bark the thick flesh of

my hands needled with splinters when I fell

into my mother's terrorful cries: ¡*Ay, Dios mio!*
I couldn't grasp her urgency: why she had to

tenderly soak my hands, as if I was some hurt
animal she had to heal, why she spent hours

pulling out every splinter with her tweezers,
a surgeon operating on me in her housecoat

and terrycloth slippers. Why her teary words:
It's okay. Just a few more, *mijo.* You could've died.

Die? I knew nothing of dying. Then she kissed
the last bead of blood on my finger, and said:

I love you. Meaning what she'd love forever
was more than my body, which suddenly split

from me into abstract breaths in the mouth
of my mind, for the first time saying to itself:

Death. Joy. Loss. Saying: I love you too, Mamá.

—playing god—

those days of my being—a naïve little god—who believed his imagination infinite in his small hands—that they could shape whatever he desired from his jumble of Lego blocks—like colorful ruins of a shattered rainbow strewn across hours of play alone in his bedroom—a lonely little god—

appealing for love through what he created—who snapped together a mini-Cadillac for his father to park in the driveway of his unaffordable dreams—who clicked together a replica of the Cuban farmhouse his

mother lost—its windows and doors in perfect proportion to her longing—a forgiving little god—who pieced together a square rose for his grandmother—though she demanded he play like real boys he'd never be—a

playful little god—who rolled rectangular cigars *made in Cuba* to light up his grandfather's memories of homeland—who forged a plastic pocketknife for his brother to stab anything he hated, even him—a mortal little god—with an immortal yearning for home—block by block he

built his perfect house scaled to his yearning, in a town he named *Richardson*, where he'd thrive someday—a frustrated little god— who tore it down back into a heap of broken rainbows he then shaped into a rocket—and blasted away toward a perfect planet he knew didn't exist—a

dejected little god—who grew up brooding over his existence—who now snaps together blocks of his melancholy words into poems—a fragile little god—still needing to be loved for what he makes, and gives of himself.

WHY I NEEDED TO

because I faithfully reply to every email from the absurd
gods of urgency who punish my good deeds by leaving me
empty when I empty my inbox . . . because I praise hating

myself, broken into my calendar's time-slotted tasks, slicing
me thin with the thick duty of being everything yet nothing
to anyone, not even to me . . . because I remember birthdays

but forget my own and my mother's . . . because she is bitter
sweet as the Cuban coffee she brews after Sunday dinners . . .
because she only loves me in the language of her cooking

my favorite dish: *carne con papas* . . . because of my bland
father sunk in his armchair without me on his lap . . . because
he never told me the life story I only read finally in the half

moons of his eyes the morning he gazed into mine then
died . . . because my brother and I need to drink to share
our shared hurt at happy hour, so unhappily grateful for

love's wreckage . . . because my husband, who's still scared
of his adoration for me as we embrace sleep, still doubts
how long I'll nest my dreams in his arms . . . because I have

never quite told him: *always* . . . because I'm just as afraid of
needing him more than myself . . . because I'm not the one
I've curated on Instagram: oh so humbled by, so grateful for . . .

so many posted blessings with my posed selves . . . because
tonight I again remember I'm nothing more than a mirage
slowly disappearing on my porch, sitting with half the life

I have left, still trying to piece how I fit into the puzzle of
the constellations . . . because I've drunk their shots of light
and too many martinis . . . because I'm cheering mindlessly

to the moon, to my wish for immortality amid the clouds
of my own cigarette smoke . . . because I should finally quit
doubting my life will be more than these anonymous bones

. . . because I need to believe in something else, truer than
me . . . because that's why today I had to take myself away
to the beach . . . because I needed to imagine my father as

that father at the shore, handing a bouquet of seashells to
his son . . . because I needed to taste that love can be simple
as a mother remembering to pack sodas and sandwiches . . .

because I needed the seagulls tending the horizon to teach
me again to be as still as them, peer calmly into the void
of the skies I face . . . because I needed to hear the waves

break and break me into the lines of this poem . . . because
I needed to burn, to see myself shine just as beautifully
as the rosy glow of the sunlight bathing my closed eyes.

UNTIL THIS:
AN EKPHRASTIC ARS POETICA

after Jacques-Louis David's
painting *The Death of Marat*

Until this poem, it was a tattoo inked with
revere on the skin of my soul. Never had I
questioned the brushed rain of silken light
falling on Marat's pallid skin. Didn't know

it was meant to illuminate a godless man
as a holy martyr faithful to the aftermath
of the French Revolution, all the textbook
pages of its horrors forgotten, dark and

muddled as the oily black layers saturating
the background, Marat bathed in his death,
slumped in his tub, an open coffin. Until
this poem, I honored the dabs of rebel red

blood oozing from his slit chest, never saw
it as a stab in rebuke for words he'd stabbed
self-righteously into all those he sentenced
to the guillotine. Until this poem, I thought

it was cordial letters he had been signing, not
death warrants, ink fresh as his blood, fingers
stiff as his quill, in his murderous hand a note
from his murderer, not a loved one. Until

this poem, I hadn't quite seen the entire canvas
of history's most constant conceit: that to love
a country justifies killing everyone who does
not love it exactly as we wish. Until this poem,

I hadn't quite believed the pen might indeed be
mightier than the sword, that the only thing
worth slaying is the end of this line, for the life
of this next one, to tell you I still want to die,

not like the Marat I now know, but the Marat
I knew when I was twelve and he opened up
to me, a glossy apparition in a coffee-table book,
when I first felt the romance of this yearning

for my last breath to be my last scribble from
a pen clutched in my hand, dying to finish one
last poem, dying for right words, dying so that
others' lives might be lived better than my own.

QUESTIONING VILLA VIZCAYA
MUSEUM AND GARDENS

Miami, Florida

To laud the spared lives of live oaks, or mourn
   the mangroves murdered for the sake of
   a tycoon's rapacious dreams of paradise?
To praise the blueprint of his vision, or curse
   the stone and marble of his palace crushing
   the native bones of the forgotten Tequesta?
To marvel through the Italian gardens, or object
   to the marshes he ordered dredged to stroll
   amid queen orchids like a Renaissance king?
To revere the regal stairs and archways, or pity
   the coral rock they were carved from, cut
   from the earth's gut, stolen for his pleasure?
To enjoy the adagio of the fountains, or dismiss
   their trickles as echoes of his bon vivant
   babble about the art he collected as chattel?
To admire his starry chandeliers, or dismiss
   them as dull ostentation, overwrought as
   his ego, as vain as his marble floors' veins?
To indulge in rooms of gilded mirrors, or crack
   them to see past my reflection, to see him
   in me, to ask him what I've asked all my life:
To create beauty, must we destroy something
   already beautiful? Does our lust for beauty
   absolve us, or does it damn us endlessly?

RADIANT BEINGS:
PHOTOS BY JOYCE TENNESON

The leathery mouths of calla lilies you kiss with
　　your lens until their mute tongues tell me:
　　we're all just as thirsty for the love of rain.

How your eye focuses a gerbera's eye, sees it as
　　the center of some sun, petals flaring with
　　my wish to color all my days pink and amber.

The perfectly crinkled faces of dahlias you blur
　　to refocus me on the letting go of beauty
　　as the truest expression of what's beautiful.

The giant heads of allium you capture teetering,
　　a lesson on how to balance the heavy weight
　　of the mind atop the stiff stem of my body.

The night you lit up with Chinese lantern flowers
　　on your dinner table, gazed at the impossible
　　glow of their orange hearts, and asked me:

Aren't they just gorgeous? As if I could say anything
　　else but *Yes!* But now I want to answer you
　　by asking: *What is it between us and flowers?*

Flowers everywhere: in the trembling hands of
　　brides, of widows, laid at granite headstones,
　　or strewn as confetti over newlyweds' beds.

Life's centerpiece at dinner parties, bouquets to
　　endear unforgiving mothers, supermarket roses
　　bought to buy back the love of angered lovers.

Orchid corsages perfuming wrists, daisy garlands
   on fairy heads, boutonnieres for the debonair,
   petunias peeking at us from window boxes.

Flowers we cut, compose as half-living sculptures
   that we place in our living rooms and praise
   every day, pining for more than our everyday.

They wilt, bow to death, and we let go, remembering
   our own fleeting flesh, hoping something of us
   might remain, radiant as the beings blooming alive
   again in your photos, in you, in me, in all of us.

—anatomy of light—

for Rafael Soriano

—across your canvases, my bones' mortal ache
is soothed by your glimmers of the immortal—
—worries wrinkled across my forehead dissolve
into the gossamer sheen of your sapphire hues—
            —I inhale the language of your gusty colors,
            exhale peaceful breaths that heal me—
            —you redraw my ribs as a divine staircase I climb back
            toward the brilliant heavens you brushed for me—
—my eyes peer within your eyes into the shadows
of all time before and after my earthly time—
            —the losses of my rock-heavy heart float amid
            the translucence of your sienna-blood clouds—
                —in your soulful colors I see myself as more
                than merely flesh, for I am the light of—
—your light that renders the infinite, that lets me stare
            at my god in the glow of your god in all humanity—

TO THE ARTIST OF THE INVISIBLE

You, whose canvas is air, who drew for me the smiles of sweet violet water, sweet as my mother's smile, dabbing, parting my hair each morning for school, her collection of perfume bottles like a miniature sculpture garden on her dresser, playing with light and time, as still as gold, patient as love waiting to be loved.

You, who sketched forever the cologne of my father's handkerchief in his suit pocket, leaving orange-blossom kisses through the house before work, only to return home, kisses of tobacco on his lips, musk around his collar.

You, with your palette of whiffs that never let my childhood end. The waxy smell of crayons still lifting off my coloring books. Sweet sniffs of pink cotton-candy clouds still floating though carnival air still smelling of roasted kettle corn. The first steamy raindrops still falling on the sidewalk the summer I learned to ride my bike. The seashell scent of my wet sandcastles still standing.

You, tracing in my mind the honeysuckle vine stitched round our kitchen window, tangled with the aromas of cumin and bay leaves circling my grandmother's stove. You, capturing that island my grandfather had to leave forever with the scents of his paradise each time he'd split open a coconut, slice into a ripe mango, hold the gold flesh to his nose and remember.

You, who draw me back into the leather of my first convertible: top-down to the night blooms of jasmine white as stars on the night my first kiss was born. Or the base notes of plumeria candles and jazz paired with top notes of merlot and sandalwood smoke the first time I knew love. Or every love that's ever left me, replaced by a portrait of scents left behind on a pillow or scarf—scents that let me forgive them.

You, the angel-wing petals of white roses and heavenly lilies praying with me at my father's wake. You keep giving me his last breath, and my first breath of Paris, my first breeze of Barcelona, my first taste of Rome, sitting alone by a fountain romancing me with the scent of wet marble.

You: magician, alchemist, artist of the invisible, who's been beside me always. Who can do what no painter or poet can do. You, who make sense of my life through scents: let me inhale it, dab it on my wrist and neck, lay it on my lapel. You, who give me all of me—for me and all to capture in a breath, like the surprise of a hummingbird that hovers midair for an instant, forever.

BIG WOOD RIVER

at Ernest Hemingway's home,
Ketchum, Idaho

Me as you, you as me, uneasy on this same terrace
      where you once sat, witnessing the same sun
you also saw rise, brushed by the same wind
      you last breathed. Now I breathe your spirit,
    my knowing you knew this river is a life,
a story that begins with tears
      of rain, or the shattered beauty of snowflakes,
fallen from faraway clouds we somehow know
      as well as ourselves, shedding the gray weight
    of our souls in whispers to the mountain peaks,
perked-up like ears needing to hear the skies,
      to feel they aren't trapped in their lovely towers,
alone. And neither are we. In the creases
      and folds of our earthen palms we collect
    our watershed into a river's voice, into a life,
into a story, letting it flow through us, urged
      ever down hills we carve with our imagination,
each freshet a sentence extending
      the story of our lives. At times clear-minded
    and tranquil, no eddies of adjective. At times
stirred, murky, stalled by declaratives of pain.
      At times the giggling of sunlight over stones,
commas that suggest a pause to listen to
      ripplings of joy. And then the rage
of whitewater rapids we fear we might not
survive. Or worse, the damming of our souls, dams
      we must break to let our stories keep

flowing downstream, new chapters
   at every bend, twisting our way through
  unknown fields. At last we reach the end of
ourselves, our stories spill as willing
  into the sea, as you did.

WHAT YOU DIDN'T LET US LOSE

for Andy Sweet

All we've lost, yet haven't, still here: in the aperture of your eyes in sync
   with your shutter opening/closing, opening/closing like heartbeats,
   letting us love what you did, see what you knew we'd never see
   again. Here: out of the darkroom of your death, the youth of
   your South Beach soul still aglow with the vintage sun of the 70's
   glinting over the ocean like some Morse code message of the past.

Here: the rays your film caught like a copper rain, still showering
   down on flowery swim caps and bathing suits before they wilted
   into today's glamour of mojitos and Maseratis along Ocean Drive.
   Here: your panorama of scattered footprints forever ingrained in
   chiseled sand, forever the same tone of tan I remember, along a
   shore that will never erode from my memory of gathering seashells
   I can still cup to my ear to hear the clicks of your camera.

Here: the pendulum of palms still swaying, keeping lost time, their
   fronds waving hello into your camera's eye, or goodbye against the
   backdrop of waves still breaking. Here: the crisp hues of perky-
   pinks, pearly-blues, and precious-mauves your lens preserved, still
   decorating Art Deco hotels frosted like birthday cakes, celebrating
   a golden age of lives your sharp focus kept from fading away.

Click: the kaleidoscopic mish-mash of lawn chairs colorful as the lives
   seated in them, the faces you zoomed in on, letting me hear their
   silent stories, epic as the horizon, wise as the wind, melancholy as
   a seagull's cry. Click: a widow still dolled up in a chiffon sundress
   and silk headscarf, still flirting with her husband's lost gaze. Click:
   a couple's leathery hands still woven together, alive in the laughter
   of each other's crinkled eyes.

Click: a grandfather still wearing his dapper golf cap, toking a cigar while dancing a polka poolside with the ladies. Click: old girlfriends kvetching, still posing like pageant contestants, though wrinkled as the ocean beyond them vanishing into its teal eternity. Click: all the Holocaust survivors who managed a smile for you, healing by forgetting—for a close-up second—what they could never forget. How you captured time, let lives live beyond their lives, shuttered immortal.

MUSIC IN OUR HANDS

after Paul Cordes's photo *The Musician*

Melodies heard are sweet, just as I heard them
in the rhythm of Keats, who thought unheard
melodies were sweeter. And so they are here, in
the silences of this musician's still hands, as if
clenched in prayer, ecstasy, or forgiveness that
his fingers, solid as pillars, can't yet release into
music, not yet strumming a guitar whispering
stars across my ears, or pounding piano keys
into my heart, not yet blowing sax smoke for
my soul, or stroking a bow across a violin like
a lover resting on his shoulder as if on mine.

His mute and empty hands are by themselves
the instrument that plays his life in tune with
mine. I imagine the thorns as well as the scents
of the faces we've held like roses in our hands,
the doughy cheeks of children we've pinched,
the cigarettes we've lit, the tears we've dabbed
from others' eyes, or from our own grieving
into the mirror, the cups of coffee we've held
beholding the sunrise, the cup of tea steeping
with the moon, the doors we've opened into
our homes, and those we've closed behind us,
forever, the days we've paused, needing to see
ourselves in the creases of our palms, to hear
all the music of our lives played out in silence.

VISITING ELIZABETH: A *GLOSA*

Is it lack of imagination that makes us come
to imagined places, not just stay at home?

———

Should we have stayed at home and thought of here?

———

Oh, must we dream our dreams
and have them, too?

—ELIZABETH BISHOP, *Questions of Travel*

—Key West | 624 White Street | 1938–1946—

I want to knock, as if the ghost of your smile, tender and restrained as your poems, awaits to greet me. I peer through the dingy windows into my reflection of you in me, imagine us sitting at your kitchen table sipping tea—no, a shot of whiskey. And I'd ask you, why you chose the blinding heat and colors of this island that I too have adored? Did you also want to dissolve into the same eternity I've seen in the sea's gaze? Did the sway of the palm trees say, as they do now: *stay, stay, stay.* And why did you leave, then? What's this glorious longing I share with you for some home we've never known, or are afraid to find? I look for answers in the questions of your poem, read it aloud at your front door as if they were *our* words: *Is it lack of imagination that makes us come / to imagined places, not just stay at home?*

—Petrópolis | Rio de Janeiro | 1951–1966—

1996: I seduced a Brazilian man into seducing me, into taking me, and taking me back to his homeland, as happened with you and your Lota decades before me. Vitorino's eyes as alluring as hers— shiny black moons in the cinnamon sky of his face. We spent that summer winding through the countryside rendered by your poems: the clouds dissipating into the samba of rain, into the dancing eddies of rivers, into the gushing roar of waterfalls, into me, wondering if you wondered: Is it the foreign that makes us feel in love, or is it love that makes us feel drawn to the foreign? After he and I made love like gods atop a mountain, I knew I could too easily let myself blur in the landscapes of his land and his life. Is that why I had to leave him? Why you couldn't leave Lota? Is that why you wrote the question I still live by: *Should we have stayed at home and thought of here?*

—North Haven Island, Maine | Summers | 1970's—

The ferry's wake cuts the bay waters that heal behind me, leaving no scar of my journey. Once docked on the island, I'll sink into the same weathered couch where you sat at the village library, caress your handwriting across the wrinkled poems you left there, brushing across your words, braille of your soul. I'll ask for directions to your house and drive, windows open, to better gaze across meadows that your eyes grazed, breathe in buttercups that perfumed your life, listen to the poetry you heard in goldfinches' chirps. I'll stand at another front door of yours, think of our lives as islands that never shift despite all we weather. But for now, what I know is the ferry's clumsy churn, the mainland shrinking into a miniature of itself until it disappears. North Haven nowhere in sight. Days later, the same will happen in reverse as I cross the bay back home. Is this why I love the sea, Elizabeth? Because it knows home is relative, something always appearing or disappearing? Because it knows the answer to paradise is the question we've both asked all our lives: *Oh, must we dream our dreams / and have them, too?*

WHAT GOVERNS US

The congress of our mountains in which I trust, upholding eons of nature's unwritten laws enacted across my eyes every dawn.

The council of our clouds that advise me on how to reshape myself, yet remain myself.

The committees of our valleys' wildflowers whose colors advise my sometimes colorless life.

I never tire of listening to the incessant debate of our waves crashing against the granite rebuttal of our coasts, neither ever wins, neither needs to, teaching me the balance of power.

The presidential stance of our pine trees that keep me loyal to our statutes of beauty reaching for the sky.

The seagulls and hawks I caucus with, who show me how to harness the shifting winds so that I can see everything, everything, even through the fog of difficult times.

At times, I think of myself afloat alone like our lone islands, yet complete and self-reliant.

Every dusk, our sovereign sun bestows across my heart its golden medal, honoring the light that beats through us all.

At night, I stare at the blank page of our moon, reminding me to never stop signing my dreams' petitions for a more just world.

I cast my vote among the twinkling senate of our stars that assemble to pass on to us our need to love as one.

We, the native who thrived here long before the foreign who sailed here. We, from away and those who have yet to arrive. We, our past, our present, our future.

We, meaning all of us who understand that what governs us is more than just ourselves.

MAINE YET MIAMI

The soft harp of snowfall plucking through
my pine trees lulls me to peace, and yet I still
       hear the bongo of thunderstorms rapping on
       the rooftop of my queer childhood, dancing
       to the rage of clouds raining away my sorrow.
Soon the snow will melt silently into the gurgles
of my creek, even as my grandmother's voice
       remains frozen in my ears, each time she'd call
       me a sissy, yet also praise me as her best friend.
I marvel over spring's abracadabra every time
the lilac blooms appear, only to disappear back
       into my grandfather's *tabaco* smoke, exhaling
       nostalgic stories about his lost Cuba, inhaling
       the scent of his jasmine tree flowering the night
       with its tiny, perfumed stars. Despite the stars
peeking through the lavender clouds swaddling
mountain peaks in my window at sunset, I rise
       to the sun of my youth rising over the sea, after
       a night's sleep on a bed of the sand, dreaming or
       dreading who I'd become, or wouldn't. Though
I grew courageous enough to marry a man who
only loves me in English: *darling, sweetheart, honey,*
       I love him in my Spanish whispered in his ear
       as he sleeps: *amorcito, tesoro, mi cielo.* After all
the meat loaves and blueberry pies we've baked
in our kitchen, I still sit down to the memories
       of my mother's table, savor my loss of her
       garlicy *fricasé de pollo* and coconut *flan.* No matter
how tastefully my throw pillows perfectly match
my knickknacks and art on my walls, it all falls

apart sometimes, just as I do, until I remember
        to be the boy I was, should always be, playing
        alone with his Legos in the family room, still
        enchanted by the joy of his sheer self and his
creations, mortal as the life I've made here.

UPON A TIME: SURFSIDE, MIAMI

Once and once again I am as I remember
myself. Thirty years later, I can still savor
the sway of these palms fanning this same
wind into syllables whispering *good morning*
in my eyes, saving these todays when I can
no longer hear how to live out this passion
for breaking myself into poems like this, like
these waves that once upon a time are again
my loyal loves still kissing my feet as I stroll
this shore and glance back at my footprints
again washed away. The salty salve of these
breezes I breathe, living once again with all
my joyous regrets for all I've done right or
wrong, for all I am now, that is enough yet
not enough, for who I wanted to be once,
still searching this sea, still facing this same
mute horizon, I ask again: *Who am I? What
should I do?* The answer, as always: *Everything.*

FROM

City of a
Hundred Fires

AMÉRICA

I.

Although Tía Miriam boasted she discovered
at least half-a-dozen uses for peanut butter—
topping for guava shells in syrup,
butter substitute for Cuban toast,
hair conditioner and relaxer—
Mamá never knew what to make
of the monthly five-pound jars
handed out by the immigration department
until my friend, Jeff, mentioned jelly.

II.

There was always pork though,
for every birthday and wedding,
whole ones on Christmas and New Year's Eve,
even on Thanksgiving Day—pork,
fried, broiled or crispy skin roasted—
as well as cauldrons of black beans,
fried plantain chips and *yuca con mojito*.
These items required a special visit
to Antonio's mercado on the corner of 8th Street
where men in *guayaberas* stood in senate
blaming Kennedy for everything—*"¡Ese hijo de puta!"*
the bile of Cuban coffee and cigar residue
filling the creases of their wrinkled lips;
clinging to one another's lies of lost wealth,
ashamed and empty as hollow trees.

III.

By seven I had grown suspicious—we were still here.
Overheard conversations about returning

to Cuba had grown wistful and less frequent.
I spoke English; my parents didn't.
We didn't live in a two-story house
with a maid or a wood-panel station wagon
nor vacation camping in Colorado.
None of the girls in our family had hair of gold;
none of my brothers or cousins
were named Greg, Peter, or Marcia;
we were not the Brady Bunch.
None of the black and white characters
on Donna Reed or on the Dick Van Dyke Show
were named Guadalupe, Lázaro, or Mercedes.
Patty Duke's family wasn't like us either—
they didn't have pork on Thanksgiving,
they ate turkey with cranberry sauce;
they didn't have *yuca,* they had yams
like the dittos of Pilgrims I colored in class.

IV.
A week before Thanksgiving
I explained to my *abuelita*
about the Indians and the Mayflower,
how Lincoln set the slaves free;
I explained to my parents about
the purple mountain's majesty,
"one if by land, two if by sea"
the cherry tree, the tea party,
the amber waves of grain,
the "masses yearning to be free"
liberty and justice for all, until
finally they agreed:
this Thanksgiving we would have turkey,
as well as pork.

V.

Abuelita prepared the poor fowl
as if committing an act of treason,
faking her enthusiasm for my sake.
Mamá set a frozen pumpkin pie in the oven
and prepared candied yams following instructions
I translated from the marshmallow bag.
The table was arrayed with gladiolus,
the plattered turkey loomed at the center
on plastic silver from Woolworths.
Everyone sat in green velvet chairs
we had upholstered with clear vinyl,
except Tío Carlos and Toti, seated
in the folding chairs from the Salvation Army.
I uttered a bilingual blessing
and the turkey was passed around
like a game of Russian roulette.
"DRY," Tío Berto complained, and proceeded
to drown the lean slices with pork fat drippings
and cranberry jelly— "*esa mierda roja,*" he called it.
Faces fell when Mamá presented her ochre pie—
pumpkin was a home remedy for ulcers, not a dessert.
Tía María made three rounds of Cuban coffee
then *abuelo* and Pepe cleared the living room furniture,
put on a Celia Cruz LP and the entire family
began to *merengue* over the linoleum of our apartment,
sweating rum and coffee until they remembered—
it was 1976 and 46 degrees—
in *América.*

LA REVOLUCIÓN AT ANTONIO'S MERCADO

Para la santera, Esperanza, who makes me open new boxes of candles so she can pick out the red ones, the color of *Changó*, her protector spirit, and tutors me in the ways of all the spirits: *Eleguá*, *Ochún*, *Yemayá*,

Para Josie on welfare, who sells me her food stamps for cash because she can't buy cocoa butter soaps, Coca-Cola, or disposable diapers with them,

Para la Señora Vidal and her husband who came early in the 50's before *la revolución*, own the famous Matador Grille on 8th Street, helped those who came later, who give me two-dollar tips when I double bag,

Para Elena who makes me sort through cartfuls of avocados to find the *best* one, her nostalgia-coated tongue complains that the fruit here can't compare to the fruit back home—where the sugar was sweeter, the salt saltier,

Para Juan Galdo who remains unsatisfied with the flavor of *los tabacos de Honduras*,

Para Mrs. Benitez the only regular who buys broccoli, who takes English night class and asks me to check her homework,

Para Pepe who asks me to translate his insurance statements, immigration papers, and junk mail offers for "free" vacations in Mexico,

Para the cashier, Consuelo, who wants me to teach her daughter María, English and love, and wants me to escort María to her *quinces* debutante,

Para Migdalia Sanchez who forgets some labels are now bilingual and comes to me confused when she mistakenly tries to read the English side of the can,

Para la vieja Gomez who I help sort through dimes, quarters and nickels—American change she has never learned to count,

Para los americanos who are scared of us, especially when we talk real loud and all at the same time, who come in only for change or to call a tow truck,

Para los haitianos who like us because at least we are Caribbean neighbors,

Para Pablito who likes his boiled ham sliced paper-thin like the after-school snacks his mother prepared for him before she was accused and sentenced,

Para Juanita who had to leave Enrique, her only son, in '61, who carries in her sequined coin purse a scratchy photo of herself at fifteen to remind herself she is still alive, and shows it to me so I can acknowledge her lost beauty,

Para Carlos who comes in mid-mornings, leans against the cafeteria counter drunk with delusion, takes a swig of espresso like a shot of whiskey and tells me *la revolución* will die before the end of the year, who hopes to host Noche Buena at his house near Havana, next year,

Para la revolución, todos sus grandes triunfos, toda su gloria,

Para Vicente my best friend, who sneaked beers with me behind the green dumpster, who taught me how to say really gross things in Spanish, who couldn't get his family out, who had only me in the States, who put a bullet through his neck on the day of his anniversary, who left a note addressed to me in Spanish—*"Para mi amigo."*

MANGO, NUMBER 61

Pescado grande was number 14, while *pescado chico* was number 12; *dinero,* money, was number 10. This was *la charada,* the sacred and obsessive numerology my *abuela* used to predict lottery numbers or winning trifectas at the dog track. The grocery stores and pawn shops on Flagler Street handed out complimentary wallet-size cards printed with the entire *charada,* numbers 1 through 100: number 70 was *coco,* number 89 was *melón* and number 61 was *mango.* Mango was Mrs. Pike, the last *americana* on the block with the best mango tree in the neighborhood. Mamá would coerce her in granting us picking rights—after all, *los americanos don't eat mango,* she'd reason. Mango was fruit wrapped in brown paper bags, hidden like ripening secrets in the kitchen oven. Mango was the perfect housewarming gift and a marmalade dessert with thick slices of cream cheese at birthday dinners and Thanksgiving. Mangos, watching like amber cat's eyes. Mangos, perfectly still in their speckled maroon shells like giant unhatched eggs. Number 48 was *cucaracha,* number 36 was *bodega,* but mango was my uncle's bodega, where everyone spoke only loud Spanish, the precious gold fruit towering in *tres-por-un-peso* pyramids. Mango was mango shakes made with milk, sugar and a pinch of salt—my grandfather's treat at the 8th Street market after baseball practice. Number 60 was *sol,* number 18 was *palma,* but mango was my father and I under the largest shade tree at the edges of Tamiami Park. Mango was Abuela and I hunched over the counter covered with the Spanish newspaper, devouring the dissected flesh of the fruit slithering like molten gold through our fingers, the nectar cascading from our binging chins, Abuela consumed in her rapture and convinced that I absolutely loved mangos. Those messy mangos. Number 79 was *cubano*—us, and number 93 was *revolución,* though I always thought it should be 58, the actual year of the revolution—the reason why, I'm told, we live so obsessively and nostalgically eating number 61's, *mangos,* here in number 87, *América.*

SHAVING

I am not shaving, I'm writing about it.
And I conjure the most elaborate idea—
how my beard is a creation of silent labor
like ocean steam rising to form clouds,
or the bloom of spider webs each morning;
the discrete mystery of how whiskers grow,
like the drink roses take from the vase,
or the fall of fresh rain, becoming
a river, and then rain again, so silently.
I think of all these slow and silent forces
and how quietly my father's life passed us by.

I think of those mornings, when I *am* shaving,
and remember him in a masquerade of foam, then,
as if it was his beard I took the blade to,
the memory of him in tiny snips of black whiskers
swirling in the drain—dead pieces of the self
from the face that never taught me how to shave.
His legacy of whiskers that grow like black seeds
sown over my cheek and chin, my own flesh.

I am not shaving, but I will tell you about the mornings
with a full beard and the blade in my hand,
when my eyes don't recognize themselves
in a mirror echoed with a hundred faces
I have washed and shaved—it is in that split second,
when perhaps the roses drink and the clouds form,
when perhaps the spider spins and rain transforms,
that I most understand the invisibility of life
and the intensity of vanishing, like steam
at the slick edges of the mirror, without a trace.

MOTHER PICKING PRODUCE

She scratches the oranges then smells the peel,
presses an avocado just enough to judge its ripeness,
polishes the McIntoshes searching for bruises.

She selects with hands that have thickened, fingers
that have swollen with history around the white gold
of a wedding ring she now wears as a widow.

Unlike the archived photos of young, slender digits
captive around black and white orange blossoms,
her spotted hands now reaching into the colors.

I see all the folklore of her childhood, the fields,
the fruit she once picked from the very tree,
the wiry roots she pulled out of the very ground.

And now, among the collapsed boxes of yucca,
through crumbling pyramids of golden mangos,
she moves with the same instinct and skill.

This is how she survives death and her son,
on these humble duties that will never change,
on those habits of living which keep a life a life.

She holds up red grapes to ask me what I think,
and what I think is this, a new poem about her—
the grapes look like dusty rubies in her hands,

what I say is this: *they look sweet, very sweet.*

THE SILVER SANDS

Before the revival of quartz pinks and icy blues
on this neon beach of Art Deco hotels and boutiques,
there were the twilight verandas lined with retirees,
the cataract eyes of Mrs. Stein who would take us
for mezzanine bingo and pancakes at Wolfie's;
I remember her beautiful orthopedic wobble.

Before sequined starlets popping out of limousine doors
and booze on the breath of every glitter-paved street,
there were the five-year-old summers of flamingo towels,
transistor radios blaring something in Spanish we ignored,
only curious of driftwood, washed-up starfish and jellyfish,
the beauty of broken conchs and our moated sandcastles.

Before the widened sidewalks and pretentious cafés
where I take my cappuccino sprinkled with cinnamon,
our mothers were peacocks in flowered bathing caps
posing for sandy Polaroids like pageant contestants;
there were fifteen-cent Cokes to their ruby lips
and there was nothing their beauty couldn't conquer.

Before the demolition of the Silver Sands Hotel,
our fathers spun dominos under the thatch-palm gazebos,
drank then insulted the scenery: *Nada like our Varadero,*
there the sand was powder; the water truly aquamarine.
I remember the poor magic of those voices—
how beautifully they remembered beauty.

324 MENDOZA AVENUE, #6

The last time I drank vodka, I drank it straight, in that chair.
You played Streisand from her famous concert in Central Park,
in '72, you said, and handed me the album cover which folded out.
I read the gloss and statistics, "largest public concert ever,"
fuzzy aerial photographs of the mob and the aftermath, beer cans,
wine bottles, wrappers, while you sang, eyes closed, to her music.

If it wasn't Streisand, you played Wonder or El Combo—always music.
The Broadway classics you reenacted from your director's chair:
West Side Story, Godspell, JC Superstar, with half a can
of root beer and a joint in the same hand, a lit Newport parked
in a garage-sale ashtray, and calla lilies that seemed to last forever
in candlelight umbra; the incense stick in the planter, almost out.

If there wasn't vodka there was usually dark rum. If not, we'd run out
to the Liquorvenient, talk small talk about clubs & Latin music
to the cashier. I'd flirt with her and get a 10% discount every time,
promising I'd pick her up later, and leave her bouncing in her chair
knowing I wouldn't be back, not for her, maybe for another six-pack
or bottle if we went dry—about 1:00 am, Enrique tapping empty cans

to a butter-knife salsa-beat and everyone waiting to use the can.
El Flaco *bongoing*, Maria *maracaing*, Roberto usually passed out
in the air-conditioned back room—something like the Central Park
album scene—and you, *one-two-threeing* on clave, controlling the music,
orchestrating the mad dancing and singing from your usual chair,
in your Chinese-red slippers, the Ghetto-Rican in you, easy as ever,

with dubbed tapes, the 45's, the vinyl jewels you've kept forever
at arms' reach. Nothing seemed to matter, not the spills or the cans,
the late rent, Kenita's health, the divorce, nor the broken dining chairs;
always a voice at 324, Elton or Puente, pop or Latin, blocking out

the off-key howls as you wrote the soundtrack, the background music
of our lives—*merengued* worries; sung blues with Holiday in the dark.

Late night, we'd pack into one car to La Palma on *la ocho*, park
at the to-go window: "*seis* Cuban sandwiches." It took forever,
but the food was our kind, the place had a native charm, its own music:
the giant neon palm, the only place to get *Materva* in ice-cold cans
at that hour; the insomniac waitress, Nilda, her bouffant all puffed-out,
and riff-raff inside the restaurant tequila'd-out and numb in their chairs.

I still stop at La Palma when I can, at a sticky table with three chairs,
I drink espresso but remember the vodka, the music, Streisand singing out
in the middle of the park and our lives, as littered as they may be, forever.

HAVANASIS

In the beginning, before God created Cuba, the earth was chaos, empty of form and without music. The spirit of God stirred over the dark tropical waters and God said, "Let there be music." And a soft *conga* began a one-two beat in the background of the chaos.

Then God called up *Yemayà* and said, "Let the waters under heaven amass together and let dry land appear." It was done. God called the fertile red earth Cuba and the massed waters the Caribbean. And God saw this was good, tapping his foot to the conga beat.

Then God said, "Let the earth sprout *papaya* and *coco* and white *coco* flesh; *malanga* roots and mangos in all shades of gold and amber; let there be *tabaco* and *café* and sugar for the *café*; let there be rum; let there be waving plantains and *guayabas* and everything tropical-like." God saw this was good, then fashioned palm trees—his pièce de résistance.

Then God said, "Let there be a moon and stars to light the nights over the Club Tropicana, and a sun for the 365 days of the year." God saw that this was good, he called the night nightlife, the day he called paradise.

Then God said, "Let there be fish and fowl of every kind." And there was spicy shrimp *enchilado,* chicken *fricasé,* cod fish *bacalao* and fritters. But he wanted something more exciting and said, "Enough. Let there be pork." And there was pork—deep fried, whole roasted, pork rinds and sausage. He fashioned goats, used their skins for bongos and *batús;* he made *claves* and *maracas* and every kind of percussion instrument known to man.

Then out of a red lump of clay, God made a Taino and set him in a city he called *Habana.* Then he said, "It is not good that Taino be alone. Let me make him helpmates." And so God created the *mulata* to dance *guaguancó* and *son* with Taino; the *guajiro* to cultivate his land and his folklore, *Cachita* the sorceress to strike the rhythm of his music, and a poet to work the verses of their paradise.

God gave them dominion over all the creatures and musical instruments and said unto them, "Be fruitful and multiply, eat pork, drink rum, make music and dance." On the seventh day, God rested from the labors of his creation. He smiled upon the celebration and listened to their music.

VARADERO EN ALBA

i. *ven*

> *tus olas roncas murmuran entre ellas*
> *las luciérnagas se han cansado*
> *las gaviotas esperan como ansiosas reinas*

We gypsy through the island's north ridge
ripe with villages cradled in cane and palms,
the raw harmony of fireflies circling about
amber faces like dewed fruit in the dawn;

the sun belongs here, it returns like a soldier
loyal to the land, the leaves turn to its victory,
a palomino rustles its mane in blooming light.
I have no other vision of this tapestry.

ii. *ven*

> *tus palmas viudas quieren su danzón*
> *y las nubes se mueven inquietas como gitanas,*
> *adivina la magia encerrada del caracol*

The morning pallor blurs these lines:
horizon with shore, mountain with road;
the shells conceal their chalky magic,
the dunes' shadows lengthen and grow;

I too belong here, sun, and my father
who always spoke paradise of the same sand
I now impress barefoot on a shore I've known
only as a voice held like water in my hands.

iii. *ven*

> *las estrellas parpadeantes tienen sueño*
> *en la arena, he grabado tu nombre,*
> *en la orilla, he clavado mi remo*

There are names chiseled in the ivory sand,
striped fish that slip through my fingers
like wet and cool ghosts among the coral,
a warm rising light, a vertigo that lingers;

I wade in the salt and time waves,
facing the losses I must understand,
staked oars crucified on the shore.
Why are we nothing without this land?

EL JAGUA RESORT

Cienfuegos Bay encroaches on the city,
its cankerous seawall carves out the shape
of an unlucky horseshoe fastened
with the remains of colonial *viviendas*
still standing like scoured sandcastles,
conquered faces peering from behind
famished columns, stucco revealing
a cryptic history in decades of chipped
cyan blue and Spanish red layers.

The *special* buses from Havana
arrive at Cienfuegos every Tuesday.
Smoked in black diesel, they deliver
batches of pale tourists in white linen
to El Jagua, a preserved 1950's resort,
where Canadians and Italians step out
drunk congas from megaphone instructions—
side-to-side, kick-then-kick, hand-to-hip;
caught in spells of *tabaco,* dark rum,
brown sugar and the young *mulatas*
who tempt the married men not like
bitches or feathered whores but like
a sea wind singing through wind chimes.
Scents of *dólares* and *dolores* around
the cracked plaster of the pool bar.

Iliana is sixteen with expired papers,
hungry and documented as "uncooperative."
Tangoed in a crepe of borrowed silk,
she dances with the ricochets of her dark curls,
promotes her *canela* flesh and crescent lips.
Iliana scatters like cinnamon powder in

the revolving eclipses over the fanned bar;
evaporates like a brush of perfume
into the inelegant lap of a French *canadiense*
whose elegant name she cannot nasal.
As Alejandro serves Habana Club & Coke—
Cuba Libre—for quarter tips, Iliana decides
on how many bars of laundry soap
or black-market trinkets to charge, hoping
he will want to pay her in cash.

Nightfalls are abrupt at El Jagua, not
the adagio witchcraft of harvest moonrises
but a quick drum slap in tandem with
the iron door slam of oceanview #634—
the tempest of Iliana naked and recanting
her faith in the lamp-light gods of her bedside;
and the opaque gods glowing from within
the strung flesh of gaping snapper mouths;
and the barefoot gods that dine on sugarwater
and sell silver pompoms of stitched fish;
and the capsized mouths of sea gods
bobbing in a poisoned bay without antidote;
and the gods hidden inside the splintered hulls
of moonlit dinghies and withered coconuts;
the gods that pull voices out of the harbor,
the gods that brew the rain and cut the cane,
the green gods that possess the palm trees;
the blaze of all the gods burning here
in this great city of a hundred fires.

FOUND LETTERS FROM 1965:
EL AÑO DE LA AGRICULTURA

I. Received by my mother from her sister,
   December 1, 1965, Cienfuegos, Cuba

"A brief letter which perhaps may be the last,
now that we have each chosen different paths.
I understand you are definitely leaving."

The glorious seventh year of *la Revolución*,
unanimously declared the year of AGRICULTURA,
the State decrees the harvests must double.
Whichever generous goddess may be,
el espíritu—the one deity in the rock
of this island who chose the *guajiro*,
and listens to *machete* prayers, listened:
out of red earth rose the canes, rose the corn;
thousands of coffee-bean eyes—the mountains saw,
the valleys yawned mouthfuls of mangos.

"Why, what else do you need, food? Not even.
You have arroz and frijoles criollos;
true, they were expensive, but . . ."

tons of sweetening *azúcar*
tons of enlivening *café*
tons of tempting *mangos*—
exports for the foreign palate,
while they let you eat *arróz y frijoles*

"I never thought you would make such a decision,
since you have never been endangered by la Revolución."

The same glorious year, the visas arrive
with the brand of a *contra-revolucionaria*.
Like the harvest, now you begin to double
into one who leaves, and one who remains.
The hands that want to leave are tired
of soaking beans, stealing sugar from the mill,
boiling vats of rice pudding for tired mouths
forced to greet friends with "*hola compañero*,"
forced to swallow the vinegar of citizen patrols.
The ears leave the whispers and speeches,
the hammer of machine guns and promises.
The eyes that want to close and run, sleep open,
against the required glossy of El Comandante,
his neo-classical hand lifted above you.
Bendito Hermes, Mercurio, Eleguá—
all gods of *los caminos*—guide you,
the hands, the ears, the eyes that leave.

"and now you so easily leave all your possessions
to your enemy—el Gobierno."

The State allows one suitcase, take anything except:
your *quinces* pin, diamond chips set in plated gold—

PROPERTY OF THE STATE

the wedding rings and Catholic saint charms,
an *azabache* pendant to protect against evil spirits—

PROPIEDAD DEL ESTADO

your *pesos cubanos* and your child's toys, gracias—

DONATIONS TO THE STATE

nudes of your son on the dresser splashing violet water,
you, posed coyly in chin-high pants mated against a palm,

black and white images of your husband in uniform peeling
from the black pages of construction paper photo albums—

MEMORIES OF THE STATE

But you search for a way to smuggle the perfume—
one part smoke of sugarcane cuttings smoldering,
two parts spray of citrus split open with incisive fingers,
one part rainfall evaporating and cane juice boiling;
three parts the rum *décimas* of *guajiro* guitars
four parts fields of mild winter skies seeded with stars—
an eau de toilette for pulses at the wrists and temples
on foreign days when you will have no language,
only the intimacy of memory's scents.

"in a strange country, you may have all you need . . .
at the price of being separated from your family
which you know you will never see again."

Primo Felipe, Tía Delia, Claudia Pérez your neighbor,
your sisters: Gloria, Tania, Alina; Rodríguez the baker;
Tío José, your brother Sergio, and your Mamá—

FAMILY OF THE STATE

II. My mother's reply to her sister,
    December 10, 1965, Cienfuegos, Cuba

"I have chosen no path, I am simply fulfilling
the destiny my life affords me."

At the end of the glorious *año* you take
the road curling away from your town,

the sugarcane fields transform into a farewell of mirrors
reflecting all the images you will never see again:
the mill clock, the reservoir, raw sugar in your hands,
your clouds, *your* moon, moving over *your* land
of polished fruits ripening on the branch,
of palm tree rustle and shadows on the ground
of coconuts hatching in a splash of splinters.
You remember you mother's eye gestures,
powdering your cheeks, penciling your eyebrows;
your father at a bowl of hot corn meal,
eating in the dignity and good silence of your home.

*"The ideas and concepts which bind family should
reign above all other concepts, religious or political."*

You reach Havana for the last time,
the mirrors recede—*el fín* of your life's reel,
a sea of still tarmac spread before you,
and a set of stairs leading into the airplane's belly.
Everything coalesces to a point, the projection
of all the gods of *la Revolución*, all the harvests,
all the years add up to the moment you cross
the platform and look back one last time
to face the retreating template of the island,
and scribble relatives' names, birth dates,
addresses, your favorite poems and flowers—
convinced that you will forget these things.
The propeller blades hum suicidally, you pause
to scan lines of the letter you've written,
the same letter I will find thirty years later,

for lies:
*"At no time have political concepts
influenced my decision to leave my country . . ."*

for fears:
"In a strange country the future is unknowable . . .
will I lose those I leave behind. . . ."

for courage:
"I hurt at the thought of separating from all of you and Mamá,
but I have chosen a husband, I have united my life,
together, our destiny leads us to another country . . ."

repeat it:
"Together, our destiny leads us to another country.
I am not the first nor the last woman
to do such a thing."

EL CUCUBANO

Lucía enjoyed the mystery, the emerald light
captive in the bright belly of *los cucubanos*
she wore clipped to her home-sewn dress
parading like a peacock at the town socials
around the reservoir and sugar mill clock.
All the *señoritas* flashed their *cucubanos*—
live pendants adorning breasts and hearts
to compete with the swirl of *guajiro* stars
for the attention of prime young caballeros
in linen *guayaberas* and straw hats;
the clock chiming every hour of courting,
denying every second of lustful thought
in the smolders of raped sugarcane fields.

Lucía knew nothing of the nerve stimulations,
the reactions that produced the bound light
of balanced chemicals in glowing abdomens.
What she knew was how the male *cucubanos*
tracked females by following their flashes;
how to trap them in Mamá's glass jars
in the mating hours of the early evening before
the moon rises strong and snuffs their glow;
how to pinch them so they cling to the dress,
near the heart, calling attention to the breasts,
the green fire silhouetting the spell of nipples.

Lucía never questioned the cool light nor Alberto
when he took her, removed her *cucubano*,
said she wouldn't be needing fireflies anymore
now that she'd belong to him and his promises.

Lucía knows how *el cucubano* swirled away
from Alberto's fingers into infinite green spirals
through palm trees and mountains, how soon after
the harvest Alberto also disappeared.
Lucía stares at stars she swears are green,
traps *cucubanos* between her cupped hands,
jade oozing between the seams of her fingers,
the phenomenon of luminescence in her palms—
light without heat, love without love.

DÉCIMA GUAJIRA

I

Veo la tierra amada
los pasos de mis padres
en estos ojos muertos
baila y canta ahora
el azúcar, la décima.

The *guajiro* arias of *la décima* drift
in the lifted dust of brackish shadows
over dancing sugarcane that follows
the meter, the rhyme, the ten-line craft
of my grandfather's melancholy gift.

II

Bajo tu manta de polvo
aquí encuentro y guardo
mi alma tallada en mármol
como un talismán de caracol
que guardo en la mano.

It is this mantle of dust that keeps
the marble music, the drifting sand
of footprints blown over this loved land;
the talismans in the hands of my sleep
that sing so slow and so very deep.

PALMITA MÍA

Así eres:
la palma libre
       de mi reposo,
la lluvia inquieta
       de tus ramas
el río que reúno
       en mis manos
y llevo a este labio
       seco e inútil,
tú, mi sed y mi agua
       mi sombra tranquila.

Así eres:
isla larga y espigada
       contigo me estiro,
mi espalda se rompe
       contra tus costas,
eres el exilio
       de mi exilio,
eres la montaña roja,
       el valle cálido
es mi boca abierta
       esperando tu cosecha.

Así eres:
la cuna verde
       el pulso
disuelto en la mano,
       un corazón de colibrí

y el centinela de estrellas,
           atenta fe
entre palmas rezando
           un credo a la brisa:
vino de coco, pan de arena
           palmita mía.

PALMITA MÍA

You are this:
the free palm
	of my rest,
the impatient rain
	from your fronds
a river I collect
	in my open hands
and bring to my dry
	useless lip,
you, my thirst, my water
	my tranquil shade.

You are this:
the drawn island lean
	I stretch with you,
my back breaks
	against your coast,
you are the exile
	of my exile
you are the red mountain,
	the temperate valley
is my mouth open
	waiting for your harvest

You are this:
the green crib
	the pulse
loose in open hand,
	a hummingbird heart

and the sentinel of still stars,
    attentive faith
among the praying palms,
    a creed of breezes:
coconut wine, loaves of sand,
    palmita mía.

Directions
to the Beach of
the Dead

TIME AS ART IN THE ETERNAL CITY

The first shadows appear like cells slowly dividing
from every tree and lamppost while my first words
divide from me onto my journal, trying to capture
how dawn light melts over the city's blank windows
and its ancient doors, opened a thousand-thousand
mornings to the sun with questions, and closed
on the moon's face without answers. All the days
that have fallen through these courtyards and alleys,
the lives that have worn these cobblestones gray,
all the gray doves that have been cast into flight
by how many church bells? After all the centuries
that have been tolled, hour by hour, and disappeared
above these domes, can it matter that I'm here now:
watching the bougainvillea blaze over the terraces,
counting on the morning to dive into the fountains,
flicker over coins, light the water up with my wishes?
Today, a temple will lose yet another stone that will
continue being a stone, and the Colosseum will move
again through its own shadow. Today, the murdered
and murderers will be remembered and forgotten,
and an empire pardoned for the sake of its beauty
in this city where time is an art. Today, a tourist
once again sits at a café with an espresso, a pen,
waiting to enter the Pantheon, waiting to gaze up
into its oculus, opening like a moonful of sunlight
in its dome, ready to stand in that beam of light,
to feel something radiant, and write it down.

A POET IN VENICE

Memory's images, once they are fixed
in words, are erased, Polo said.
Perhaps I am afraid of losing Venice
all at once, if I speak of it.

—ITALO CALVINO, *Invisible Cities*

Unlike others, he arrives feeling the train whistling
through him, aware of every step on the platform
and the clatter of trailing his suitcase and his lust
for beauty across the station's rusting shadows
to the laps of water, which he imagines as kisses.

He strolls across footbridges, feels the pageantry
of the cherubs and marble scrolls under his feet.
Above him, the laundry lines turn into rainbows
strung between bare windows laced with violets,
he compares their petals to tears of Murano glass.

On postcards he begins his poems: *Everything*
speaks to me here, even the brass eyes of the lions
on the door knockers. In my window, the palazzi
rise like cliffs, enduring the tug of the sea's memory,
the pull of the moon. Today at the Ducale I will . . .

At the Ducale he imagines himself as a prisoner
crossing the Bridge of Sighs into the dungeons,
carving his name in a wall before dying, believes
this is just as beautiful as the rows of market fruit,
the blood plums he takes pictures of, and devours.

He tastes the Adriatic, craves his warm loneliness
and abandons the map he's carried like a prayer

book, loses himself among the names of saints
until every street ends with his reflection running
into the watercolors of the city over the canals.

Lost in a *campo,* sitting on a granite bench under
the iron swirls of gas lamps and glow of pink glass
blushing the night, he notices the flames flicker
with stray giggles, whispers carried on the wind.
He follows the ricochet of footsteps with his ears,

leading him to the groan of empty gondola hulls,
to the creak of shutters, imagines them closing
like eyelids, and Venice a lover he can't possess
asleep at his side dreaming without him, his eyes
wading alone through the wide-open darkness.

because the winds are too strong, our Captain announces, his voice like an oracle coming through the loudspeakers of every lounge and hall, as if the ship itself were speaking. We're not going to Malta— *an enchanting island country fifty miles from Sicily,* according to the brochure of the tour we're not taking. But what if we did go to Malta? What if, as we are *escorted on foot through the walled "Silent City" of Mdina,* the walls begin speaking to me; and after we *stop a few minutes to admire the impressive architecture,* I feel Malta could be *the* place for me. What if, as we *stroll the bastions to admire the panoramic harbor and stunning countryside,* I dream of buying a little Maltese farm, raising Maltese horses in the green Maltese hills. What if, after we *see the cathedral in Mosta saved by a miracle,* I believe that Malta itself is a miracle; and before I'm *transported back to the pier with a complimentary beverage,* I'm struck with Malta fever, discover I am *very* Maltese indeed, and decide I must return to Malta, learn to speak Maltese with an English (or Spanish) accent, work as a Maltese professor of English at the University of Malta, and teach a course on The Maltese Falcon. Or, what if when we *stop at a factory to shop for famous Malteseware,* I discover that making Maltese crosses is my true passion. Yes, I'd get a Maltese cat *and* a Maltese dog, make Maltese friends, drink Malted milk, join the Knights of Malta, and be happy for the rest of my *Maltesian* life. But we're not going to Malta. Malta is drifting past us, or we are drifting past it—an amorphous hump of green and brown bobbing in the portholes with the horizon as the ship heaves over whitecaps wisping into rainbows for a moment, then dissolving back into the sea.

SOMEWHERE TO PARIS

*The sole cause of a man's unhappiness is that
he does not know how to stay quietly in his room.*

—PASCAL, *Pensées*

The *vias* of Italy turn to memory with each turn
and clack of the train's wheels, with every stitch
of track we leave behind, the *duomos* return again
to my imagination, already imagining Paris—
a fantasy of lights and marble that may end
when the train stops at Gare de l'Est and I step
into the daylight. In this space between cities,
between the dreamed and the dreaming, there is
no map—no legend, no ancient street names
or arrows to follow, no red dot assuring me:
you are here—and no place else. If I don't know
where I am, then I am only these heartbeats,
my breaths, the mountains rising and falling
like a wave scrolling across the train's window.
I am alone with the moon on its path, staring
like a blank page, shear and white as the snow
on the peaks echoing back its light. I am this
solitude, never more beautiful, the arc of space
I travel through for a few hours, touching
nothing and keeping nothing, with nothing
to deny the night, the dark pines pointing
to the stars, this life, always moving and still.

TORSOS AT THE LOUVRE

after Rilke

These are your clavicles balancing what's left
of your shoulders, jutting into the ghostly air
like the persistent nubs of broken-off wings.

This is the face of your chest facing the world,
seeing and speaking for you now, in a language
of forms that have nothing to do with words.

This is your back: accurate, precise, and loyal,
refusing to let its posture go, holding you up
in place, as if you were still completely whole.

These marble veins are your veins flowing
from a heart of stone, the last part that will
crumble, once every part of you has failed

you, unarmed warrior, blind hunter, or lover
without hands or lips—this is you, after you
and all you were meant to be, life beyond

a face, name, or history—no longer struggling
to change what we cannot change, almost free
of the greed of the mind and deeds of the body.

AFTER BARCELONA, IN BARCELONA

After hearing nothing through seven centuries
rising from candles into sooty eyes of *santos*
fixed in the weeping stone of cathedral walls,
after my obsession over the wrinkled hands
of gray couples walking in ascots and pearls
up Passeig Gracia every night into oblivion,
after taking down three days of notes, I take
el metro down to La Arena on la Gran Via,
don't ask if it's gay or straight at the door,
just pay my Euros, get stamped, don't care
if it's techno or trance, or that it's teen night
and I'm thirty-four. I bracket my elbows back
on the bar, not dancing, just watching, thinking
if there's a poem in this city, it's not hanging
in the galleries of Miró's colors, but right here
in the ecstasy of these *kids* dancing in the rain
of red, green, and blue lights over their tattoos.
Not in the rows of Picasso portraits, but here:
these post-modern faces with pierced eyebrows
and bodies grooving in three dimensions at once,
their egos hanging at the end of their cigarettes,
their bell-bottoms dragging the floor in defiance
of their youth that will outlive me, and this city
that will outlive us both. After turning every alley
into a sentence, after hunting through the market
for a kilo of similes, after stirring metaphors over
espressos, waiting for the city to *speak*, tonight
I stand in a poem that isn't mine, but theirs.

DIRECTIONS TO THE
BEACH OF THE DEAD

Go to Europe, go to Spain, in Barcelona, walk
under centuries hanging from the iron lamps
of the Gothic Quarter. Touch the mossy walls
down a Venetian-width street until you reach
La Rambla, move with the drove to the Mercat,
but don't touch the plums stacked in pyramids
nor the apples layered like red bricks, don't stare
at the eyes of lamb heads on ice. Buy a cheap map
vanish into Plaça Catalunya and study the anatomy
of the subway lines flowing under the city's skin.
Take the red one to Sants, count out three Euros
in your palm, buy a RENFE ticket south and wait.
Get on. Ride past the fringe of factories, past
the dusky windows, the laundry on the balconies
of the Catalans who make and serve the *chorizos*,
paellas, and *pimientos*—all the *tapas* you've tasted.

At km-per-hour, listen to piped-in Ravel and Bach
above the clack of tracks through tunnels of rock.
You'll emerge riding the edge of cliffs cantilevered
over the Mediterranean. Pull out your map, follow
the towns' names lettered straight out into the sea
like their piers in Catalán: Castelldefels, Gavá, Prat de
Llobregat where Dalí pictured a Madonna protecting
the port, blessing the trade of goods, watching evil.
Minutes before Sitges, recite Lorca who lived there:
verde que te quiero verde / verde que te quiero verde / verde . . .
though it's not very green at all, you'll ask yourself:
Should I live here? Could I live here? Don't answer—
just get off at Sitges, trickle south from the station
through the capillary of boutique streets, tempting
you with nothing you need. Go on: buy perfumes,

silks, silver rings, sandals you'll wear to walk up
to the city's *catedral* like a fort against the beach.
Wait for the bells and gulls, light a candle, then go—
follow the promenade, past El Hotel Terramar,
past empty stone benches like old men facing
the sea, thinking of places they may never see.

After the promenade, listen for the steel rails
vibrating like a tuning fork still humming from
the pass of the last train. Walk on the tracks until
you reach a small mountain. Smell the names
of flowers you've never known, take pictures
against the wind as you climb up, then down into
a crescent-shaped cove. Take your sandals off,
knead your soles over moon-white stones until
you can't walk anymore, take off your clothes,
lie down between the sun and earth, fall asleep—
past Sitges and Barcelona, past Europe, yourself.
Let the breeze wake you, feel the waves push, pull
at your feet, then take a stone, weigh it in your hand,
bring it to your lips—throw it in, throw another and
another, try to fill the sea with stones, and you will
understand why, la Platjes del Mort, la Playa del Muerto,
the beach where you stand, is named for the dead.

WINTER OF THE VOLCANOES: GUATEMALA

Because rain clouds shade the valley all summer,
they call this their winter, and I'm here, witness
to the rains of August, surrounded by volcanoes.
Volcanoes everywhere, like cathedrals at the end
of every stretch of cobblestone I wobble through.
Volcanoes, triangulating the view in every window,
reading over my shoulders on the terrace at night,
funneling stars between their peaks, threatening
to grumble and leave *la Antigua* to rise a third time
out of ruin. Volcanoes, keeping watch like a council
of four unforgiving gods: Acatenango, Fuego, Agua,
and Pacaya—the one I climbed, step by step through
rows of corn groomed like manes by Mayan hands,
through the quilt work of terrace farmers' patches,
through clouds veiling through pinewood forests,
until I walked in pumice fields, barren as the moon,
if the moon were black, spelled out my name with
freshly minted stones I laid down to claim: *I was here*
on this newly kilned rock that in a few eons will be
the soil of the valley, the earth I savor in my coffee,
the dust settling over windowsills and counter tops.
I scaled the peak, reached the crater's lip, stood silent
over the cauldron of molten, blood-orange petals,
the pearlescent fire, an open wound weeping smoke,
terrified I might fall, terrified that, for a moment,
I'd let myself be seduced by the pure, living heart
of the raw earth, saying: *here, let me take you back.*

BARGAINING WITH A GODDESS
(AT THE CHICHI MARKET, GUATEMALA)

after Rigoberta Menchú

The diversity of materials, techniques, and designs
of these Guatemalan products enables the nation's
artisans to satisfy the most discerning tastes.

—VISITE GUATEMALA 2001

Jade rosaries and letter openers, little jaguars on key rings, paperback copies of the ancient Popol Vuh, shelves lined with plastic temples, wooden saints, rows of black Christs with hand-painted eyes looking toward heaven, and a woman the color of a dry rose, fanning her skirt, showing me a frenzy of hummingbirds and mountain flowers embroidered in colors truer than my life. *Algo para your wife?* she asks, leading me to her table where she riffles through her pile of skirts like a flipbook of flora and fauna. But I'm not married. *O, then algo for your casa* she orders, shuffling through her placemats, stacking them like tortillas, insisting I examine the threads of her exquisite stitching—*Mira, mira—only 20 quetzales for you.* I pay what she asks, knowing there is more to her, more than I can know or bargain for: silver bangles and crucifixes, wooden saints staring into the air, streams of *copal* incense drifting into faces, bags of fresh rose petals laid out like candy, and hollow piñatas swaying in the shadows of the market. But how much for the reds, greens, and yellows of her valley, for her ancient rows of corn, for her Christian sins, her bleeding knees and *promesas?* How much for her gods that commanded her flesh out of corn, for her thoughts in Quiché, her forgotten astrology and eons of history? How much for her cloud forests, her rain, for her ruins and her village, for her candlelit home and raw wool blankets? How much for the magic of her needles blossoming flowers somewhere inside the folds of these mountains no one can own, under a breadth of priceless stars even my imagination cannot buy?

RETURN FROM *EL CERRADO*

for V.C.L.

Two days ago, I was below the equator and you
were driving, holding the wheel with one hand, and
my hand with the other. It was summer on the road,
iron-red dust lifting like a ghost, and I was hoping
this: that I belonged wherever I was going with you,
north into the Amazon or south toward São Paulo—
I couldn't tell, it was all green to me, it was all acres
of sky-filled lakes, all waterfalls and streams tearing
through the mountains, it was all mountains, it was
about you and me and the possibility, the odds of
disappearing into you, into your country, into one
of its villages with gables and bell towers peeking
through the landscape. I'd get used to the blooms
bursting through October, frost glazing over July,
you'd teach me Portuguese, I'd teach you Spanish:
mão is *mano, pan* is *pão, amanhã* is *mañana,* but today
I'm at the woodgrain of my desk again with nothing
changed: the same bouquet of pen-n-pencil stems,
the furniture unmoved, the same color on the walls,
the same books on sagging shelves, and winter here,
a season away from you, a continent against me.

SILENT FAMILY CLIPS

The projector whirls like a tiny, black time machine
on the coffee table, a cone of light shoots the dark,
opens a hole in the living room wall like a portal
into lives I never knew, years I don't remember living.
1970 is about ten seconds long featuring a version
of my brother I never loved, content with hitting
a ball against the graffiti on a city wall, twenty years
before we'd learn to be brothers | the wall breaks
to Miami Beach waves dissolving at my *abuela's* feet,
sauntering down the shore with beauty pageant steps,
her bathing cap flowers fresh as the Art Deco facades
shimmering behind her | fading away to my *abuelo*
standing on the boardwalk at orthodox attention,
his hair once as black as the black of his oxfords,
the circles from his *tabaco* like tree rings dating him
and filling the frame with smoke | the smoke clears
to a mist floating above Niagara Falls, the deluge
a backdrop to a woman who must be my mother,
donning a magenta blouse scribbled with paisleys,
a string of plastic teal beads like a candy necklace
competing against the golden mums and the clock
in a knot garden where she's never been a widow
standing next to Papá | he speaks into the camera,
but the film is silent, cloud shadows darken over
his dark lips, a voice I can't hear forever | forever
there is a room strung with banners and balloons,
a birthday cake circled by faces like stained glass
lit by dim candlelight, faces not yet loved or lost
by a boy who is me | I watch myself close my eyes,
take a breath, make a wish I will never remember.

PAPÁ'S BRIDGE

Morning, driving west again, away from the sun
rising in the slit of the rearview mirror, as I climb
on slabs of concrete and steel bent into a bridge
arcing with all its parabolic y-squared splendor.
I rise to meet the shimmering faces of buildings
above treetops meshed into a calico of greens,
forgetting the river below runs, insists on running
and scouring the earth, moving it grain by grain.

And for a few inclined seconds every morning
I am twelve years old with my father standing
at the tenth-floor window of his hospital room,
gazing at this same bridge like a mammoth bone
aching with the gravity of its own dense weight.
The glass dosed by a tepid light reviving the city
as I watched and read his sleeping, wondering
if he could even dream in such dreamless white:

Was he falling? Was he flying? Who was he, who
was I underneath his eyes, flitting like the birds
across the rooftops and early stars wasting away,
the rush-hour cars pushing through the avenues
like the tiny blood cells through his vein, the I.V.
spiraling down like a string of clear licorice feeding
his forearm, bruised pearl and lavender, colors
of the morning haze and the pills on his tongue.

The stitches healed, while the room kept sterile
with the usual silence between us. For three days
I served him water or juice in wilting paper cups,
flipped through muted soap operas and game shows,

and filled out the menu cards stamped Bland Diet.
For three nights I wedged flat and strange pillows
around his bed, his body shaped like a fallen S
and mortared in place by layers of stiff percale.

When he was ordered to walk, I took his hand,
together we stepped to the window and he spoke
—*You'll know how to build bridges like that someday*—
today, I cross this city, this bridge, still spanning
the silent distance between us with the memory
of a father and son holding hands, secretly in love.

WHAT'S LOVE GOT TO DO?

All summer Papá holds a cigarette out the window of his laser-green Buick, points his lips left to blow the smoke into the mirage of exhaust between rush hour cars. All summer he listens to *La Cubanisima* on AM radio exploding with accounts of how Castro took everything *we* had, how *we'd* get it back someday. All summer he wears polyester ties and his over-polished loafers. All summer I float my arm like a wing out the window as we glide down Coral Way, past storefronts and memories: the 7-11 stops for Blow-Pops and Slurpees, the square pizzas at Frankie's, the birthday dinners at Canton Rose. All summer I want to ask if he remembers what I remember, but I don't, so he just drives, all summer, keeping a safe distance in the right lane, from our Miami suburb to my uncle's *bodega*, where all summer I price and rotate, mop and bag and save for my own car. All summer I don't want to be me. I don't want to be my father either, eleven years in his windowless office adding and subtracting, wishing and forgetting he could be more. All summer he picks me up at 6:00 and we drive back on the same road, the same mix of cigarettes and Piña Colada air freshener, the same visors eclipsing our faces, the same silence. All summer I wait for him to say something—anything, like: *I hate grapefruit juice,* or *I can't stand the Navarros,* or *I've cheated on your mother,* or *I hate this life.* What he does say is: *I love Tina Turner,* every time I took control of the radio and tuned in to her #1 hit on FM. All summer he sings along in his thick Cuban accent *(waus love gotta do / gotta do wis it)* and whistles through the words he didn't know. Then he smiles saying something about Mamá and him in the 60's dancing to Ike and Tina in Cuba, and picks up the refrain again *(waus love but a secon' hand emoshun).* All summer, embarrasses me with his singing, that summer, before his throat swells, before his weekly visits to Dr. Morad, before the Mitomycin and Hail Marys fail, before I never hear him sing again. That summer, when all I manage to mutter back at him is: *Yeah, I love Tina, too.*

VISITING METAPHORS AT SOUTH POINT

Light has begun to taper toward the sun, the day
drawn out of the sky, hooded over the pier planks
reaching into the horizon like a wooden keyboard
veneered with dead fish scales glinting in silver leaf.
I stand like the piles, tending my shadow, which is
twice as long as it was twenty-five years ago when
I stood here with no metaphors for these images
of light that was just light, your face only itself—
a wordless profile beside me, but enough for a son:
to have his father's hand curled around his finger,
to creak down the pier together, not looking for
philosophy in the eyes of fishermen gutting fish,
nor trying to read the smears of blood like graffiti.
Enough to be just a boy on a Saturday, belonging
to my father, to reach the end of the pier, meet
the simple thrill of wanting to jump in the water,
before it became the sea talking back in similes,
before silence itself became a figure of speech for you.
Enough to brave the jetty with you holding me
as I leaned over jagged rocks, watching jellyfish
fade in-and-out of the water's lens, years before
I would compare their weak and deliberate pulses
to your final breaths, their vanishing to your death.

TRANSLATION FOR MAMÁ

What I've written for you, I have always written
in English, my language of silent vowel endings
never translated into your language of silent h's.
> *Lo que he escrito para ti, siempre lo he escrito*
> *en inglés, en mi lengua llena de vocales mudas*
> *nunca traducidas a tu idioma de haches mudas.*
I've transcribed all your old letters into poems
that reconcile your exile from Cuba, but always
in English. I've given you back the *guajiro* roads
you left behind, stretched them into sentences
punctuated with palms, but only in English.
> *He transcrito todas tus cartas viejas en poemas*
> *que reconcilian tu exilio de Cuba, pero siempre*
> *en inglés. Te he devuelto los caminos guajiros*
> *que dejaste atrás, transformados en oraciones*
> *puntuadas por palmas, pero solamente en inglés.*
I have recreated the *pueblecito* you had to forget,
forced your green mountains up again, grown
valleys of sugarcane, stars for you in English.
> *He reconstruido el pueblecito que tuviste que olvidar,*
> *he levantado de nuevo tus montañas verdes, cultivado*
> *la caña, las estrellas de tus valles, para ti, en inglés.*
In English I have told you how I love you cutting
gladiolas, crushing *ajo*, setting cups of *dulce de leche*
on the counter to cool, or hanging up the laundry
at night under our suburban moon. In English,
> *En inglés te he dicho cómo te amo cuando cortas*
> *gladiolas, machacas ajo, enfrías tacitas de dulce de leche*
> *encima del mostrador, o cuando tiendes la ropa*
> *de noche bajo nuestra luna suburbana. En inglés*

I have imagined you surviving by transforming
yards of taffeta into dresses you never wear,
keeping Papá's photo hinged in your mirror,
and leaving the porch light on, all night long.
>   *He imaginado cómo sobrevives transformando*
>   *yardas de tafetán en vestidos que nunca estrenas,*
>   *la foto de Papá que guardas en el espejo de tu cómoda,*
>   *la luz del portal que dejas encendida, toda la noche.*
>   *Te he captado en inglés en la mesa de la cocina*
>   *esperando que cuele el café, que hierva la leche*
>   *y que tu vida se acostumbre a tu vida. En inglés*
>   *has aprendido a adorar tus pérdidas igual que yo.*
I have captured you in English at the kitchen table
waiting for the *café* to brew, the milk to froth,
and your life to adjust to your life. In English
you've learned to adore your losses the way I do.

THE PERFECT CITY CODE

for M.C.

1(a)   Streets shall be designed *Euro–Style* with 300-ft right-of-ways, benches, and flowered traffic circles, to provide a distinct sense of beauty, regardless of cost.

1(b)   There shall be a canopy of trees; these shall be your favorite: *Giant Royal Palms*, 25-ft high, whereas their fronds shall meet in cathedral-like arches with a continuous breeze that shall slip in our sleeves and flutter against our bodies so as to produce angel-like sensations of eternity.

1(c)   There shall be bushes; these shall also be your favorite: *Tea Roses* @ 2-ft o.c. to provide enough blooms for casual picking; whereas said blooms shall spy on us from crystal glasses set next to the stove, over coffee-table books, or in front of mirrors.

2(a)   Sidewalks shall be crack-proof and 15-ft wide for continuous, side-by-side conversations; painted either a) *Sunflower Brown,* b) *Mango Blush,* or c) *Rosemont Henna*; whereas such colors shall evoke, respectively: the color of your eyelashes, of your palms, the shadows on your skin.

3(a)   There shall be an average of one (1) Parisian–style café per city block, where I shall meet your eyes, dark as espresso, above the rim of your demitasse, and hold your hand like a music box underneath the table; where we shall exercise all those romantic, cliché gestures we were always too smart for.

3(b)   There shall also be one (1) open-air market per city block to facilitate the purchase of tulips, raspberries, white chocolate baci, and other gourmet items to lavish our lives; whereas every night I shall watch you through a glass of brandy as you dice fresh cilantro and dill, disappearing into the scent steaming around you.

4(a)   Utility poles or structures that obstruct our view shall not be permitted. At all times we shall have one of the following vistas: birds messaging across the sky, a profile of mountains asleep on their backs, or a needlepoint of stars.

5(a)   There shall be an *Arts District* and we shall float through gallery rooms on Saturday afternoons perplexed by the pain or conflict we can't feel in a line or a splatter of color; works that glorify or romanticize tragedy shall not be allowed.

5(b)   There shall also be a *Historic District* to provide residents with a distinct sense of another time. We shall live there, in a loft with oak floors, a rose-marble mantle where our photos will gather; our years together will compete with the age of the brick walls and cobblestones below our vine-threaded balcony.

(*)   Without exception, there shall be a central square with a water fountain where we shall sit every evening by the pageantry of cherubs; where we shall listen to the trickle of their coral mouths; where I shall trust the unspoken; where you shall never again tell me there's nothing here for you, nothing to keep you, nothing to change your mind.

WHEN I WAS A LITTLE CUBAN BOY

O *José can you see* . . . that's how I sang it, when I was
a *cubanito* in Miami, and *América* was some country
in the glossy pages of my history book, someplace
way north, everyone white, cold, perfect. *This Land
Is My Land,* so why didn't I live there, in a brick house
with a fireplace, a chimney with curlicues of smoke.
I wanted to wear breeches and stockings to my *chins,*
those black pilgrim shoes with shiny gold buckles.
I wanted to eat yams with the Indians, shake hands
with *los negros,* and dash through snow I'd never seen
in a one-horse hope-n-say? I wanted to speak in British,
say really smart stuff like *fours core and seven years ago*
or *one country under God, in the visible.* I wanted to see
that land with no palm trees, only the strange sounds
of flowers like petunias, peonies, impatiens, waiting
to walk through a door someday, somewhere in *God
Bless America,* and say, *Lucy, I'm home, honey. I'm home.*

LOOKING FOR BLACKBIRDS, HARTFORD

Your postcard from Varadero Beach is on my dresser at home,
where the surf of it rolls day and night making mild Cuban sounds.

—WALLACE STEVENS in a letter to José Rodriguez Feo

8/16
Ladies in charcoal and pink Chanel suits
sip hot chai from glass mugs at Michael's.
They mind the afternoon with eyes fixed
on the side of their faces, like blackbirds.

10/14
The rose-thatched gazebo at Elizabeth Park
has bared itself into a cloud of thorny vines
where even blackbirds do not perch.

11/1
Along a row of *Perfect-Six* townhomes,
a woman matted by a field of red brick
caws out from a third story window like
a blackbird wanting other blackbirds.

12/19
Near the end of fall the black leaves
look like feathers strewn over lawns.

12/21
After the first snowfall nothing remains
black, not even the night. Nothing breaks
the white reverence, not even a blackbird.

1/5

The reservoir has hardened into a bed of ice
expanding, groaning. It's the only sound I hear
complaining of winter through the mountain.

1/28

Airplanes pass, their shadows like blackbirds
landing on the snowy fields before the runway.

2/3

The buildings downtown stand like chess pieces
in a stalemate against the frozen riverfront
that will not break until a blackbird flies.

2/24

The Portuguese men in heavy black coats
gather like blackbirds at La Estrella heckling
over Old World days and the World Cup.

3/18

All the bakery cases along Franklin Avenue
in Little Italy, glitter with sprinkled cannoli,
anise candies, and iced cookies. But no pies.

4/2

At the bus stop on Park and Main, I catch
hummingbirds hovering in the rainforest eyes
of *puertorriqueños*. Where are my *pájaros negros*?

4/13

On the telephone lines dripping with snow
in my window, there ought to be blackbirds,
they ought to be slitting the sky wide open.

HOW CAN YOU LOVE NEW YORK?

Do you buy white chrysanthemums and tangelos
at your favorite Korean corner every Thursday,
leave them in an alley you've ignored too long
and say: surprise my little apple pie, I love you?
Or *cab it* to Chinatown on a Saturday morning
and ask the woman with marquise-shaped eyes
behind the Pearl River counter adding your bill
in Cantonese, to come spend the night with you?
Do you kiss the Chelsea boys on the lips, grab
their bulging Diesel jeans and say goddamn it,
I love this town. Is New York a gorgeous man,
or a stunning woman you take uptown to dinner
and compliment the way her long, silky black
avenues fall across her streets? After how many
brie and San Pellegrino picnics in Central Park,
and shows at the MOMA, do you decide it's love,
but it's just not going to work, without therapy?
How many times will you have to raise your eyes
from garbage, flyers, and gum blotches to the sky
scrapers, and scream, I forgive you NY, NY for
cussing at me and shoving me, for trying to take
over my life, for not listening or calling me back?
How many nights will you spend thinking it over
with the rain sheer as the vodka in your martini,
looking out a bar window at the mélange of lights
floating over the wet pavement with possibilities?
What makes you believe this is it, this is *the* one
you can lose yourself to forever and never want
to leave? How do you know the city isn't lying?

NO MORE THAN THIS, PROVINCETOWN

Today, home is a cottage with morning
in the yawn of an open window. I watch
the crescent moon, like a wind-blown sail,
vanish. Blue slowly fills the sky and light
regains the trust of wildflowers blooming
with fresh spiderwebs spun stem to stem.
The room rises with the toasting of bread,
a stick of butter puddling in a dish, a knife
at rest, burgundy apples ready to be halved,
a pint of blueberries bleeding on the counter,
and little more than this. A nail in the wall
with a pair of disembodied jeans, a red jersey,
and shoes embossed by the bones of my feet
and years of walking. I sit down to breakfast
over the nicks of a pinewood table and I am,
for a moment, not afraid of being no more
than what I hear and see, no more than this:
the echo of bird songs filling an empty vase,
the shadow of a sparrow moving through
the shadow of a tree, disturbing nothing.

CROSSING BOSTON HARBOR

The horn blares—once—twice—sounding like
iron, a dull and heavy slap across the wind's face.

And if the wind could have a face, it would resemble
these strangers, blank as paper dolls propped up

against the railing as the propeller torque vibrates
through the vessel, slowly peeling the hull away

from the barnacled dock, the limp ropes coiled
like dry roses on the metal deck, the anchor up

like a rusty bow hung on the bow, and we move
all together, at the same speed, to the same point.

The ferry's chine makes an incision across the bay,
its churned waters bleed a wake of lustrous blue

behind us as we head west, scanning the coastline
nested with gables and fringed with flocked sails,

their peaks waning out of sight into memory, until
there's nothing left to measure our distance against.

So much of my life spent like this—suspended,
moving toward unknown places and names or

returning to those I know, corresponding with
the paradox of crossing, being nowhere yet here,

leaning into the wind and light, uncertain of what
I might answer the woman to my right, anchored

in a flutter of cottons and leaning over the stern,
should she lift her eyes from the sea toward me

and ask: *So, where are you from?*

MEXICAN ALMUERZO IN NEW ENGLAND

for M.G.

Word is praise for Marina, up past 3:00 a.m. the night before her flight, preparing and packing the *platos tradicionales* she's now heating up in the oven while the *tortillas* steam like full moons on the stove top. Dish by dish she tries to recreate Mexico in her son's New England kitchen, taste-testing *el mole* from the pot, stirring everything: *el chorizo-con-papas, el picadillo, el guacamole.* The spirals of her stirs match the spirals in her eyes, the scented steam coils around her like incense, suffusing the air with her folklore. She loves Alfredo, as she loves all her sons, as she loves all things: *seashells, cacti, plumes, artichokes.* Her hand calls us to circle around the kitchen island, where she demonstrates how to fold tacos for the *gringo* guests, explaining what is *hot* and what is *not,* trying to describe tastes with English words she cannot savor. As we eat, she apologizes: *not as good as at home, pero bueno* . . . It is the best she can do in this strange kitchen which Sele has tried to disguise with *papel picado* banners of colored tissue paper displaying our names in piñata pink, maíz yellow, and Guadalupe green—strung across the lintels of the patio filled with talk of an early spring and *do you remembers* that leave an aftertaste even the *flan* and *café negro* don't cleanse. Marina has finished. She sleeps in the guest room while Alfredo's paintings confess in the living room, while the papier-mâché skeletons giggle on the shelves, and shadows lean on the porch with rain about to fall. Tomorrow our names will be taken down and Marina will leave with her empty clay pots, feeling as she feels all things: *velvet, branches, honey, stones.* Feeling what we all feel: home is a forgotten recipe, a spice we can find nowhere, a taste we can never reproduce, exactly.

WHERE IT BEGINS — WHERE IT ENDS

somewhere
the wind blows and
a mountain is pared down
a cliff's chin is shaved
a dune is stolen from a desert
a parched field is raped
ripe stones are ground
weathered into souls
and dead things burn alive
into ghosts of gray ash
almost invisible, arriving
from places I've never been

somehow
the dust sweeps in
through a cracked window
underneath the front door
and comes to rest on my desk
over the edge of a frame
on blocks of consumed books
over an array of aging photos
gingerly settling out of beams
in the morning light, floating
in the quite air of my room
until the wind blows again

Looking for
The Gulf Motel

LOOKING FOR THE GULF MOTEL

Marco Island, Florida

There should be nothing here I don't remember . . .

The Gulf Motel with mermaid lampposts
and ship's wheel in the lobby should still be
rising out of the sand like a cake decoration.
My brother and I should still be pretending
we don't know our parents, embarrassing us
as they roll the luggage cart past the front desk
loaded with our scruffy suitcases, two-dozen
loaves of Cuban bread, brown bags bulging
with enough mangos to last the entire week,
our espresso pot, the pressure cooker—and
a pork roast reeking garlic through the lobby.
All because we can't afford to eat out, not even
on vacation? Only two hours from our home
in Miami, but far enough away to be thrilled
by *whiter* sands on the *west* coast of Florida,
where I should still be for the first time watching
the sun set instead of rise over the ocean.

There should be nothing here I don't remember . . .

My mother should still be in the kitchenette
of The Gulf Motel, her daisy sandals from Kmart
still squeaking across the linoleum, still gorgeous
in her teal swimsuit and amber earrings
stirring a pot of *arroz con pollo*, adding sprinkles
of onion powder and dollops of tomato sauce.
My father should still be in a terrycloth jacket
smoking, clinking a glass of amber whiskey

in the sunset at The Gulf Motel, watching us
dive into the pool, two sons he'll never see
grow into men who will be proud of him.

There should be nothing here I don't remember . . .

My brother and I should still be playing *Parcheesi*,
my father should still be alive, slow dancing
with my mother on the sliding-glass balcony
of The Gulf Motel. No music, only the waves
keeping time, a song only their minds hear
ten thousand nights back to their life in Cuba.
My mother's face should still be resting against
his bare chest like the moon resting on the sea,
the stars should still be turning around them.

There should be nothing here I don't remember . . .

My brother should still be thirteen, sneaking
rum in the bathroom, sculpting naked women
from sand. I should still be eight years old
dazzled by seashells and how many seconds
I hold my breath underwater—but I'm not—
I am thirty-eight, driving up Collier Boulevard,
looking for The Gulf Motel, for everything
that should still be, but isn't. I want to blame
the condos, their shadows, for ruining the beach,
and my past, I want to chase the snowbirds away
with their tacky mansions and yachts, I want
to turn the golf courses back into mangroves.
I want to find The Gulf Motel exactly as it was
and pretend for a moment, nothing lost is lost.

BETTING ON AMERICA

My grandmother was the bookie, set up
at the kitchen table that night, her hair
in curlers, pencil and pad jotting down
two-dollar bets, paying five-to-one
on which Miss would take the crown.

Abuelo put his money on Miss Wyoming—
She's got great teeth, he pronounced as if
complimenting a horse, not her smile
filling the camera before she wisped away
like a cloud in her creamy chiffon dress.

I dug up enough change from the sofa
and car seats to bet on Miss Wisconsin,
thinking I was as American as she because
I was as blond as she was. And I knew
that's where all the cheese came from.

That wasn't all: chocolate was from Miss
Pennsylvania, the capital of Miss Montana
was Helena, Mount Rushmore was in
Miss South Dakota, and I knew how to say
Miss *Con-nec-ti-cut,* unlike my Tía Gloria

who just pointed at the TV: *Esa—that one,*
claiming she had her same figure before
leaving Cuba. *It's true . . . I have pictures,*
she declared before cramming another
bocadito sandwich into her mouth.

Papá refused to bet on any of the Misses
because *Americanas all have skinny butts,*
he complained. *There's nothing like a big
culo cubano.* Everyone agreed—*es verdad*—
except for me and my little cousin Julito,

who apparently was a breast man at five,
reaching for Miss Alabama's bosom
on the screen, the leggy *mulata* sashaying
in pumps, swimsuit, seducing Tío Pedro
into picking her as the sure winner.

She's the one! She looks Cubana, he swore,
and she did, but she cost him five bucks.
¡Cojones! he exploded as confetti rained,
Bert Parks leading Miss Ohio, the new
Miss America, by the hand to the runway.

Gloves up to her elbows, velvet down
to her feet, crying diamonds into her bouquet,
the queen of *our* country, *our* land of the free,
amid the purple mountains of her majesty
floating across the stage, our living room,

though no one bet on her, and none of us
—not even me—could answer Mamá
when she asked: *¿Dónde está Ohio?*

TAKING MY COUSIN'S PHOTO
AT THE STATUE OF LIBERTY

for Roxana

May she never miss the sun or the rain in the valley
trickling from Royal palms, or the plush red earth,
or the flutter of sugarcane fields and poincianas, or
the endless hem of turquoise sea around the island,
may she never remember the sea or her life again
in Cuba selling glossy postcards of the revolution
and *El Che* to sweaty Germans, may she never forget
the broken toilet and peeling stucco of her room
in a government-partitioned mansion dissolving
like a sandcastle back into the Bay of Cienfuegos,
may she never have to count the dollars we'd send
for her wedding dress, or save egg rations for a cake,
may she be as American as I wanted to be once, in love
with its rosy-cheeked men in breeches and white wigs,
with the calligraphy of our *Liberty and Justice for All,*
our *We the People,* may she memorize all fifty states,
our rivers and mountains, sing "God Bless America"
like she means it, like she's never lived anywhere
else but here, may she admire our wars and our men
on the moon, may she believe our infomercials, buy
designer perfumes and underwear, drink Starbucks,
drive a Humvee, and have a dream, may she never
doubt America, may this be her country more than
it is mine when she lifts her Diet Coke like a torch
into the June sky and clutches her faux Chanel purse
to her chest, may she look into New York Harbor
for the rest of her life and hold still when I say, *Smile.*

THE ISLAND WITHIN

for Ruth Behar

I'm still thinking about your porch light
like a full moon casting a foggy halo
in the frigid air last night, the bare oaks
branching into the sky like nerve endings
inches away from the frozen stars,
the pink gables of your Victorian home
protesting yet another winter for you
captive in Ann Arbor as you practice
mambo by the fireplace. I'm following
your red-velvet shoes to conga beats
and bongo taps taking your body, but
not your life, from the snow mantling
your windows outside, 1,600 miles
away from Cuba. I'm tasting the *cafecito*
you made, the slice of homemade flan
floating in burnt sugar like the stories
you told me you can't finish writing,
no matter how many times you travel
through time back to Havana to steal
every memory ever stolen from you.

You're a thief anyone would forgive,
wanting only to imagine faces for names
chiseled on the graves of your family
at Guanabacoa, walk on Calle Aguacate
and pretend to meet the grandfather
you never met at his lace shop for lunch,
or pray the Kaddish like your mother
at the synagogue in El Vedado, stand
on the steps there like you once did

in a photo you can't remember taking.
I confess I pitied you, still trying to reach
that unreachable island within the island
you still call home. I thought I was done
with Cuba, tired of filling in the blanks,
but now I'm not sure. Maybe if I return
just once more, walk the sugarcane fields
my father once cut, drive down the road
where my mother once peddled guavas
to pay for textbooks, sit on the porch
of my grandmother's house, imagine her
still in the kitchen making *arroz con leche*—
maybe then I'll have an answer for you
last night when you asked me: *Would you
move to Cuba? Would you die there?*

PRACTICE PROBLEM

If I leave home at 12:48 pm, drive
8 miles, catch a plane accelerating
at 3 m/s^2 against the earth spinning
900 mph clockwise, and count

76 Royal palms from the sky before
I land in Havana at exactly 3:28 pm,
if I take a bus through rain falling
at 15° and cross a 1,500-foot bridge

between two mountains where
my mother was born at 6:52 am,
if I get off the bus, head south
at 36 mph in a '57 Buick with a tail

wind blowing off the sugarcane
south by southeast at 18 ft/s
to my grandfather's town where
I see the same 4,701 stars he saw

above his house, if I suddenly
decelerate at 2 m/s^2 to follow
a man in a straw hat for a mile
because he looks like my father,

if I turn around, walk 3,200 steps
per day, how long will it take me
to get back home knowing I have
1.2 billion seconds left to live?

EL FLORIDA ROOM

Not a study or a den, but *El Florida*
as my mother called it, a pretty name
for the room with the prettiest view
of the lipstick-red hibiscus puckered up
against the windows, the tepid breeze
laden with the brown-sugar scent
of loquats drifting in from the yard.

Not a sunroom, but where the sun
both rose and set, all day the shadows
of banana trees fan-dancing across
the floor, and if it rained, it rained
the loudest, like marbles plunking
across the roof under constant threat
of coconuts ready to fall from the sky.

Not a sitting room, but *El Florida,* where
I sat alone for hours with butterflies
frozen on the polyester curtains
and faces of Lladró figurines: sad angels,
clowns, and princesses with eyes glazed
blue and gray, gazing from behind
the glass doors of the wall cabinet.

Not a TV room, but where I watched
Creature Feature as a boy, clinging
to my brother, safe from vampires
in the same sofa where I fell in love
with Clint Eastwood and my *abuelo*
watching westerns, or pitying women
crying in telenovelas with my *abuela.*

Not a family room, but the room where
my father twirled his hair while listening
to eight-tracks of Elvis, read Nietzsche
and Kant a few months before he died,
where my mother learned to dance alone
as she swept, and I learned salsa pressed
against my Tía Julia's enormous hips.

At the edge of the city, in the company
of crickets, beside the empty clothesline,
telephone wires, and the moon, tonight
my life sits with me like an old friend
not in the living room, but in the light
of El Florida, as quiet and necessary
as any star shining above it.

AFTERNOONS AS ENDORA

I'm a boy who hates being a boy who loves cats and paint-by-number sets. She's a witch who loves being a witch who hates mortals. Every afternoon she pops in on channel six on top of a lampshade or a banister, and I disappear behind the locked door of my bedroom. I paint my fingernails crayon-red, wrap a towel around my head like her bouffant, tie my sheets around my chest into a chiffon muumuu just like hers, the bedspread draped over my shoulders like her mauve cape. We give *Derwood* cat-eye scowls and scoff at Samantha's patience with mortal fools. In our raspy voices we cast spells turning Mrs. Kravitz into a Chihuahua and the boys at recess into ants I can squish. With a flick of our wrists we puncture the milkman's truck tires and conjure up thunderstorms to rain out baseball practice. With a wave of our billowy sleeves we give Larry Tate amnesia and trick my mother into signing me up for art classes. We brew bat's wings with eyes of newt into potions to make me like girls and my father a little more. We turn my grandmother into a mute so she can't scream at me: *Go play outside! Don't be such a sissy! Talk like a man, will you?* For thirty minutes we sit on clouds, drink bubbly brews from cognac glasses, gaze into a crystal ball at my wonderful future until—poof—she disappears in a cloud of smoke, leaving me alone in my room again, the boy afraid of being a boy, dressed like a witch, wanting to vanish too.

QUEER THEORY: ACCORDING TO
MY GRANDMOTHER

Never drink soda with a straw—
      los machos shouldn't use straws—
      (for milk shakes, maybe).
Stop eyeing your mother's Avon catalog,
and the men's underwear in those Sears flyers.
      I've seen you . . .
Stay out of her Tupperware parties,
and perfume bottles—don't let her kiss you,
      she kisses you much too much.
Avoid hugging men, but if you must,
      pat them real hard
      on the back, even
      if it's your father.
Must you keep that cat? Don't pet him so much.
      Mijo, why don't you like dogs?
Never play house, even if you're the husband.
Quit hanging with that Henry kid, he's too pale,
      and I don't care what you call them—
      those GI Joes of his
      are dolls.
Don't draw rainbows or flowers or sunsets.
      I've seen you . . .
Don't draw at all—no coloring books either.
Put away your crayons, your Play-Doh, your Legos.
      Where are your Hot Wheels,
      your laser gun and handcuffs,
      those knives I gave you
      for Christmas?
Never fly a kite or roller skate, but light
all the firecrackers you want,
kill all the lizards you can, cut up worms—
feed them to that damn cat of yours.

Don't sit Indian style with your legs crossed—
        you're no *indio*.
Stop click-clacking your sandals—
        you're no Tropicana chorus girl.
And for God's sake, never pee sitting down.
        I've seen you . . .
Never take a bubble bath or wash your hair
with shampoo—*el champú* is for women.
        So is conditioner.
        So is *el mousse*.
        So is hand lotion.
Never file your nails or blow-dry your hair—
go to the barber shop with your *abuelo*—
        you're not *unisex*, are you?
Stay out of the kitchen. *Los hombres* don't cook—
they eat. Eat anything you want, except:
        deviled eggs
        Blow-Pops
        croissants (bagels, maybe)
        cucumber sandwiches
        and those girly petit-fours
Don't watch *Bewitched* or *I Dream of Jeannie*.
Don't stare at *The Six-Million Dollar Man*.
        I've seen you . . .
Never dance alone in your room:
Donna Summer, Barry Manilow, The Captain
and Tennille, Bette Midler—all musicals—
        forbidden.
Posters of kittens, Star Wars, or the Eiffel Tower—
        forbidden.
Those fancy books on architecture and art—
        I threw them in the trash.
You can't wear cologne or puka shells
and I better not catch you in clogs.
If you grow a ponytail—I'll cut it off.

¡Qué! No way, you can't pierce your ear,
  left *or* right side—
  I don't care—
you will not look like some god-damn queer—
  I've seen you . . .
even though I know
   you *are* one.

MAYBE

for Craig

Maybe it was the billboards promising
paradise, maybe those fifty-nine miles
with your hand in mine, maybe my sexy
roadster, top down, the wind fingering
your hair, the sunlight on your thighs
and bare chest, maybe it was just the ride
over the sea split in two by the highway
to Key Largo, or the *idea* of Key Largo.
Maybe I was finally in the right place
at the right time with the right person.
Maybe there'd finally be a house, a dog
named Chu, a lawn to mow, neighbors,
dinner parties, and you, forever obsessed
with crossword puzzles and Carl Jung,
reading in the dark by the moonlight,
at my bedside every night. Maybe. Maybe
it was the clouds paused at the horizon,
the blinding fields of golden sawgrass,
the mangrove islands tangled, inseparable
as we might be. Maybe I should've said
something, promised you something,
asked you to stay a while. Maybe.

THICKER THAN COUNTRY

A Cuban like me living in Maine? Well,
what the hell, Mark loves his native snow
and I don't mind it, really. I even love
icicles, though I still decorate the house
with seashells and starfish. Sometimes
I want to raise chickens and pigs, wonder
if I could grow even a small mango tree
in my three-season porch. But mostly,
I'm happy with hemlocks and birches
towering over the house, their shadows
like sundials, the cool breeze blowing
even in the summer. Sometimes I miss
the melody of Spanish, a little, and I play
Celia Cruz, dance alone in the basement.
Sometimes I miss the taste of white rice
with *picadillo*—so I cook, but it's never
as good as my mother's. Why don't I miss
her or the smell of Cuban bread as much
as I should, I wonder? But when Mark
comes home like an astronaut dressed
in his ski clothes, or when I spy on him
planting petunias in the spring, his face
smudged with this earth, or barbequing
in the summer when he asks me if I want
a *hamberg* or a *cheezeberg* as he calls them—
still making me laugh after twelve years—
I understand why the mountains here
are enough, white with snow or green
with palms, mountains are mountains,
but love is thicker than any country.

KILLING MARK

His plane went down over Los Angeles
last week (again), or was it Long Island?
Boxer shorts, hair gel, his toothbrush
washed up on the shore at New Haven,
but his body never recovered, I feared.

Monday, he cut off his leg chain sawing—
bled to death slowly while I was shopping
for a new lamp, never heard my messages
on his cell phone: *Where are you? Call me!*
I told him to be careful. He never listens.

Tonight, fifteen minutes late, I'm sure
he's hit a moose on Route 26, but maybe
he survived, someone from the hospital
will call me, give me his room number.
I'll bring his pajamas, some magazines.

5:25: still no phone call, voice mail full.
I turn on the news, wait for the report:
flashes of moose blood, his car mangled,
as I buzz around the bedroom dusting
the furniture, sorting the sock drawer.

Did someone knock? I'm expecting
the sheriff by six o'clock. *Mr. Blanco,
I'm afraid* . . . he'll say, hand me a Ziploc
with his wallet, sunglasses, wristwatch.
I'll invite him in, make some coffee.

6:25: I'll have to call his mom, explain,
arrange to fly the body back. Do I have
enough garbage bags for his clothes?
I *should* keep his ties—but his shoes?
Order flowers—roses—white or red?

By seven-thirty I'm taking mental notes
for his eulogy, suddenly adorning all
I've hated, ten years' worth of nose hairs
in the sink, of lost car keys, of chewing
too loud and hogging the bedsheets,

when Joey yowls, ears to the sound
of footsteps up the drive, and darts
to the doorway. I follow with a scowl:
Where the hell were you? Couldn't call?
Translation: *I die each time I kill you.*

COOKING WITH MAMÁ
IN MAINE

Two years since trading mangos
for these maples, the white dunes
of the beach for the White Mountains
etched in my living room window,
I ask my mother to teach me how
to make my favorite Cuban dish.

She arrives from Miami in May
with a parka and a suitcase packed
with plantains, chorizos, *vino seco*,
but also onions, garlic, olive oil
as if we couldn't pick these up at
the Oxford County Hannaford's.

She brings with her all the spices
of my childhood: laurel, *pimentón*,
dashes of memories she sprinkles
into a black pot of black beans
starting to simmer when I wake up
and meet her busy in the kitchen.

With my pad and pencil, eager
to take notes, I ask her how many
teaspoons of cumin she's adding,
how many cups of oil and *vino seco*
but I can't get a straight answer:
I don't know, she says, *I just know.*

Afraid to stay in the guest cottage,
by herself, but not of the blood
on her hands, she stabs holes
in the raw meat, stuffs in garlic:
*Six or seven mas ó menos, maybe
seven cloves*, she says, *it all depends.*

She dices *about* one bell pepper,
tells me how much my father loved
her cooking too, as she cries over
about two onions she chops, tosses
into a pan sizzling with olive oil
making *sofrito* to brown the roast.

She insists I just watch her hands
stirring, folding, whisking me back
to the kitchen I grew up in, dinner
for six of us on the table, six sharp
every day of her life for thirty years
until she had no one left to cook for.

I don't ask how she survived her *exilio*:
ten years without her mother, twenty
as a widow. Did she grow to love snow
those years in New York before Miami,
and how will I survive winters here with
out her cooking? Will I ever learn?

I savor answers to my questions when
she raises a spoon to my mouth saying,
Taste it, mijo, there's no recipe, just taste.

MY FATHER IN MY HANDS

My father gave me these hands, fingers
inch-wide and muscular like his, the same
folds of skin like squinted eyes looking
back at me whenever I scrub them
in the kitchen sink and remember him
washing garden dirt off his, or helping
my mother dry the dishes every night.

These are his fingernails—square, flat—
ten small mirrors I look into and see him
signing my report card, or mixing batter
for our pancakes on Sunday mornings.
His same whorls of hair near my wrists,
magnetic lines that pull me back to him
tying my shoelaces, pointing at words
as I learned to read, and years later:
greasy hands teaching me to change
the oil in my car, immaculate hands
showing me how to tie my necktie.

These are his knuckles—rising, falling
like hills between my veins—his veins,
his pulse at my wrist under the watch
he left for me, ticking after his death,
alive whenever I hold a man's hand and
remember mine around my father's thumb
all through the carnival at Tamiami Park,
how he lifted me up on his shoulders,
his hands wrapped around my ankles
keeping me steady above the world, still.

SINCE UNFINISHED

I've been writing this since
the summer my grandfather
taught me how to hold a blade
of grass between my thumbs
and make it whistle, since
I first learned to make green
from blue and yellow, turned
paper into snowflakes, believed
a seashell echoed the sea,
and the sea had no end.

I've been writing this since
a sparrow flew into my class
and crashed into the window,
laid to rest on a bed of tissue
in a shoebox by the swings, since
the morning I first stood up
on the bathroom sink to watch
my father shave, since our eyes
met in that foggy mirror, since
the splinter my mother pulled
from my thumb, kissed my blood.

I've been writing this since
the woman I slept with the night
of my father's wake, since
my grandmother first called me
a faggot and I said nothing, since
I forgave her and my body
pressed hard against Michael
on the dance floor at Twist, since
the years spent with a martini
and men I knew couldn't love.

I've been writing this since
the night I pulled off the road
at Big Sur and my eyes caught
the insanity of the stars, since
the months by the kitchen window
watching the snow come down
like fallout from a despair I had
no word for, since I stopped
searching for a name and found
myself tick-tock in a hammock
asking nothing of the sky.

I've been writing this since
spring, studying the tiny leaves
on the oaks dithering like moths,
contrast to the eon-old fieldstones
unveiled of snow, but forever
works-in-progress, since tonight
with the battled moon behind
the branches spying on the world—
same as it ever was—perfectly
unfinished, my glasses and pen
at rest again on the night table.

I've been writing this since
my eyes started seeing less,
my knees aching more, since
I began picking up twigs, feathers,
and pretty rocks for no reason
collecting on the porch where
I sit to read and watch the sunset
like my grandfather did every day,
remembering him and how
to make a blade of grass whistle.

How to Love
a Country

COMO TÚ / LIKE YOU / LIKE ME

for the D.A.C.A. DREAMers and all our nation's immigrants

. . . my veins don't end in me   *. . . mis venas no terminan en mí*
but in the unanimous blood   *sino en la sange unánime*
of those who struggle for life . . .   *de los que luchan por la vida . . .*

—ROQUE DALTON, *Como tú*

Como tú, I question history's blur in my eyes
each time I face a mirror. Like a mirror, I gaze
into my palm a wrinkled map I still can't read,
my lifeline an unnamed road I can't find, can't
trace back to the fork in my parents' trek
that cradled me here. *Como tú,* I woke up to
this dream of a country I didn't choose, that
didn't choose me—trapped in the nightmare
of its hateful glares. *Como tú,* I'm also from
the lakes and farms, waterfalls and prairies
of another country I can't fully claim either.
Como tú, I am either a mirage living among
these faces and streets that raised me here,
or I'm nothing, a memory forgotten by all
I was taken from and can't return to again.

Like memory, at times I wish I could erase
the music of my name in Spanish, at times
I cherish it, and despise my other syllables
clashing in English. *Como tú,* I want to speak
of myself in two languages at once. Despite
my tongues, no word defines me. Like words,
I read my footprints like my past, erased by
waves of circumstance, my future uncertain
as wind. Like the wind, *como tú,* I carry songs,

howls, whispers, thunder's growl. Like thunder,
I'm a foreign-borne cloud that's drifted here,
I'm lightning, and the balm of rain. *Como tú*,
our blood rains for the dirty thirst of this land.
Like thirst, like hunger, we ache with the need
to save ourselves, and our country from itself.

COMPLAINT OF EL RÍO GRANDE

for Aylin Barbieri

I was meant for all things to meet:
to make the clouds pause in the mirror
of my waters, to be home to fallen rain
that finds its way to me, to turn eons
of loveless rock into lovesick pebbles
and carry them as humble gifts back
to the sea which brings life back to me.

I felt the sun flare, praised each star
flocked about the moon long before
you did. I've breathed air you'll never
breathe, listened to songbirds before
you could speak their names, before
you dug your oars in me, before you
created the gods that created you.

Then countries—your invention—maps
jigsawing the world into colored shapes
caged in bold lines to say: you're here,
not there, you're this, not that, to say:
yellow isn't red, red isn't black, black is
not white, to say: *mine*, not *ours*, to say
war, and believe life's worth is relative.

You named me big river, drew me—blue,
thick to divide, to say: *spic* and *Yankee*,
to say: *wetback* and *gringo*. You split me
in two—half of me *us*, the rest *them*. But
I wasn't meant to drown children, hear
mothers' cries, never meant to be your
geography: a line, a border, or murderer.

I was meant for all things to meet:
the mirrored clouds and sun's tingle,
birdsongs and the quiet moon, the wind
and its dust, the rush of mountain rain—
and us. Blood that runs in you is water
flowing in me, both life, the truth we
know we know as one in one another.

LEAVING IN THE RAIN:
LIMERICK, IRELAND

for Caroline

I have no exact reason to miss you, your city, nor
this island of yours—like everything, like nothing
I had imagined: the plentiful wisdom of so much
silver rain softening rock, spreading across pillows
of green hills rolling past the train's window leaving
Limerick after only a few days of knowing you, and
my life with your kin, teaching myself by teaching
them to trust a poem's imagery, hear it as music
enough to mend what we ourselves rend apart.

I smiled your smile, answering me: *No, lad, limericks*
didn't come from here. Yet I felt poetry everywhere:
in the brooding walls of King John's Castle against
your grey sky, in the daring of a few rays of sunlight
each day striking the steel and glass of my hotel,
in the granite sparkle of sidewalks solid under foot
on our daily lunchtime strolls to Dunnes for bacon
and pears, also bread to court the seagulls gathered
every afternoon by the River Shannon, its tidal ebb
and flow a recurring dream, you noticed, reminding
me to remember and forget myself twice each day.

Why should your home be home to me? My eyes
belong to another sea, my feet to another island—
Cuba, where rain falls differently. Yet the stranger
on the train across the aisle could be my mother
pulling turquoise yarn from a tote bag on the floor
like a faithful dog sitting beside her swollen ankles.
Her long needles, a soft, rhythmic whetting of steel

against steel, could be a cello in her spotted hands
that don't remember or need her anymore to make
what: socks for her granddaughter, another sweater
for her faraway son, a vest for her dead husband?
Only she knows what she misses, what is, was, or will
be home to her, knows the sorrow in her every stitch
as much as the joy pulled from each loop she purls.

Beside her, a bearded man sleeps, his furrowed brow
and bony hands tell a story like the broken spine
of the book facedown on his lap, parted to words
he couldn't finish—too droll or terrifying for him,
perhaps. I wonder if his eyes are green as ferns
or brown as dirt, if they're dreaming of tigers, or
moonlight echoes, or the timbre of his father's voice.
I wonder if he's leaving home or returning. Maybe
he's a stranger like me, among strangers between
points on the earth to which these tracks are nailed.
Where am I? Where am I going? It doesn't matter.

What matters is the poem in the window: a blurred
watercolor where tree is chimney, chimney is cloud,
cloud is brick, brick is puddle, puddle is rain, and rain
is me, refracted in each luscious bead. How free and
impossible to be everything inside everything I see.
How terribly beautiful never having to say I'm from
here or *there*, never recalling my childhood home
where I played checkers alone, or the royal palms
lining the street where I learned to ride my bike,
or my mango-scented backyard catching fireflies
like stars in glass jars, or my bedroom where I first
heard my voice say, *Richard*, my name breaking
me from the world, the world suddenly broken
into geography, history, weather, language, war.

I would like to die twice, Caroline: once to feel
that last breath flood my body, then come back
to tell of life not pulled apart, not dimensioned—
a seamless mass at light-speed before the dead
stop of the train at 3:05. Before the man wakes up,
closes his book, forgets or vows to live his dream.
Before the woman stuffs her needles into her bag,
stands up, sighs into the ache of her feet. Before
everything becomes itself again: brick into brick,
tree into tree, cloud into cloud, puddle into puddle,
me into me, standing on the platform knowing
Pavese was right: *You need a village, if only for
the pleasure of leaving it . . .* and someday returning
to it, to your city, to you, and the rain we shared.

ISLAND BODY

Forced to leave home, but home
never leaves us. Wherever exile
takes us, we remain this body made
from the red earth of our island—
our ribs taken from its *montes*—
its breeze our breaths. We stand
with its *palmeras*. Our eyes hold
its blue-green sea. Waterfalls
echo in our ears. On our wrists,
jasmine. Our palms open, close
like its hibiscus to love, be loved.

We thrive wherever we remain
true to our *lucha*—the hustle
of our feet walking to work
as we must, our oily hands
fixing all the broken beauty
we must fix, our soiled hands
growing what we must grow,
or cutting what must be cut,
our backs carrying the weight
of our island's sands, our pulse
its waves, our sweat the gossamer
dew and dust of its sunrises,
our voice the song of its *sinsontes*
and its *son* nested in our souls.

Wherever the world spins us,
home remains the island that
remains in us. Its sun still sets
in our eyes, its clouds stay still

above us, our hands still hold
its tepid rain. We're still caught
under its net of stars, still listen to
its moon crooning above its dirt
roads. We're its rivers, the hem
of its coast and lace of its *sierras*,
its valley windsongs, its vast seas
of green sugarcane fields. We're
our island's sweetness as bitter
as the taste of having to leave it.

MATTERS OF THE SEA

US Embassy Reopening Ceremony,
Havana, Cuba, August 14, 2015

The sea doesn't matter, what matters is this:
we all belong to the sea between us, all of us
once and still the same child who marvels over
starfish, listens to hollow shells, sculpts dreams
into impossible castles. We've all been lovers,
holding hands, strolling either of our shores—
our footprints like a mirage of selves vanished
in waves that don't know their birth or care
on which country they break. They break, bless
us, return to the sea, home to our silent wishes.

No one is other, to the other, to the sea, whether
on hemmed island or vast continent, remember:
our grandfathers, their hands dug deep into red
or brown earth, planting maple or mango trees
that outlived them; our grandmothers counting
years while dusting photos of their weddings—
brittle family faces still alive on *our* dressers now.
Our mothers teaching us how to read in Spanish
or English, how to tie our shoes, how to gather
fall's colors, or bite into guavas. Our fathers worn
by the weight of clouds, clocking-in at factories,
or cutting sugarcane to earn a new life for us.
My cousins and I now scouting the same stars
above skyscrapers or palms, waiting for time
to stop and begin again when rain falls, washes
its way through river or street, back to the sea.

No matter what anthem we sing, we've all walked
barefoot and bare-souled among the soar and dive
of seagull cries. We've offered our sorrows, hopes
up to the sea, our lips anointed by the same spray
of salt-laden wind. We've fingered our memories
and regrets like stones in our hands we can't toss.
Yet we've all cupped seashells to our ears. Listen
again to the echo—the sea still telling us the end
to our doubts and fears is to gaze into the lucid blues
of our shared horizon, breathe together, heal together.

MOTHER COUNTRY

To love a country as if you've lost one: 1968,
my mother leaves Cuba for America, a scene
I imagine as if standing in her place—one foot
inside a plane destined for a country she knew
only as a name, a color on a map, or glossy photos
from drugstore magazines, her other foot anchored
to the platform of her *patria*, her hand clutched
around one suitcase, taking only what she needs
most: hand-colored photographs of her family,
her wedding veil, the doorknob of her house,
a jar of dirt from her backyard, goodbye letters
she won't open for years. The sorrowful drone
of engines, one last, deep breath of familiar air
she'll take with her, one last glimpse at all
she'd ever known: the palm trees wave goodbye
as she steps onto the plane, the mountains shrink
from her eyes as she lifts off into another life.

To love a country as if you've lost one: I hear her
—*once upon a time*—reading picture books
over my shoulder at bedtime, both of us learning
English, sounding out words as strange as the talking
animals and fair-haired princesses in their pages.
I taste her first attempts at macaroni-n-cheese
(but with chorizo and peppers), and her shame
over Thanksgiving turkeys always dry, but countered
by her perfect pork *pernil* and garlic *yuca*. I smell
the rain of those mornings huddled as one under
one umbrella waiting for the bus to her ten-hour days
at the cash register. At night, the *zzz-zzz* of her sewing
her own blouses, *quinceañera* dresses for her nieces

still in Cuba, guessing at their sizes, and the gowns
she'd sell to neighbors to save for a rusty white sedan—
no hubcaps, no air conditioning, sweating all the way
through our first vacation to Florida theme parks.

To love a country as if you've lost one: as if
it were *you* on a plane departing from America
forever, clouds closing like curtains on your country,
the last scene in which you're a madman scribbling
the names of your favorite flowers, trees, and birds
you'd never see again, your address and phone number
you'd never use again, the color of your father's eyes,
your mother's hair, terrified you could forget these.
To love a country as if I was my mother last spring
hobbling, insisting I help her climb all the way up
to the US Capitol, as if she were here before you today
instead of me, explaining her tears, her cheeks pink
as the cherry blossoms coloring the air that day when
she stopped, turned to me, and said: You know, *mijo*,
it isn't where you're born that matters, it's where
you choose to die—that—that's your country.

MY FATHER IN ENGLISH

First half of his life lived in Spanish: the long syntax
of *las montañas* that lined his village, the rhyme
of *sol* with his soul—a Cuban *alma*—that swayed
with *las palmas*, the sharp rhythm of his *machete*
cutting through *caña*, the syllables of his *canarios*
that sung into *la brisa* of the island home he left
to spell out the second half of his life in English—
the vernacular of New York City sleet, neon, glass—
and the brick factory where he learned to polish
steel twelve hours a day. Enough to save enough
to buy a used Spanish-English dictionary he kept
bedside like a bible—studied fifteen new words
after his prayers each night, then practiced them
on us the next day: *Buenos días, indeed, my family.*
Indeed más coffee. Have a good day today, indeed—
and again in the evening: *Gracias to my bella wife,*
indeed, for dinner. Hiciste tu homework, indeed?
La vida is indeed difícil. Indeed did indeed become
his favorite word which, like the rest of his new life,
he never quite grasped: overused and misused often
to my embarrassment. Yet the word I most learned
to love and know him through: *indeed,* the exile who
tried to master the language he chose to master him,
indeed, the husband who refused to say *I love you*
in English to my mother, the man who died without
true translation. *Indeed,* meaning: in fact/*en efecto,*
meaning: in reality/*de hecho,* meaning to say now
what I always meant to tell him in both languages:
thank you/*gracias* for surrendering the past tense
of your life so that I might conjugate myself here
in the present of this country, in truth/*así es, indeed.*

EL AMERICANO IN THE MIRROR

Maybe you don't remember, or don't want to, or
maybe, like me, you've never been able to forget:
May 1979, fifth-grade recess, I grabbed your collar,
shoved you up against the wall behind the chapel,
called you a sissy-ass *americano* to your face, then
punched you—hard as I could. Maybe you still live,
as I do, with the awful crack of my knuckles' slam
on your jaw, and the grim memory of your lip split.

Why didn't you punch me back? That would've hurt
less than the jab of your blue eyes dulled with pain—
how you let your body wilt, lean into me, and we
walked arm in arm to the boys' room, washed off
the blood and dirt. Is that how you remember it?
What you can't remember is what I thought when
our gazes locked in the mirror and I wanted to say:
I'm sorry, maybe *I love you*. Perhaps even kiss you.

Did you feel it, too? At that instant did we both
somehow understand what I'm only now capable
of putting into these words: that I didn't hate you,
but envied you—the *americano* sissy I wanted to be
with sheer skin, dainty freckles, the bold consonants
of your English name, your perfectly starched shirts,
pleated pants, that showy *Happy Days* lunchbox,
your A-plus spelling quizzes that I barely passed.

Why didn't you snitch on me? I don't remember now
who told Sister Magdalene, but I'll never forget how
she wrung my ears until I cried for you, dragged me

to the back of the room, made me stand for the rest
of that day, praying the rosary to think hard about
my sins. And I did, I have for thirty-two years, Derek.
Whether you don't remember, don't want to, or never
forgot: forgive me, though I may never forgive myself.

USING COUNTRY IN A SENTENCE

My chair is *country* to my desk. The empty page
     is *country* to my lifelong question of *country*
turning like a grain of sand irritating my mind, still
     hoping for some pearly answer. My question
is *country* to my imagination, reimagining *country*,
     not as our stoic eagle, but as wind, the *country*
its feathers and bones must muster to soar, eye
     its kill of mice. The wind's *country* as the clouds
it chisels into hieroglyphs to write its voice across
     blank skies. A mountain as *country* to the clouds
that crown and hail its peak, then drift, betray it
     for some other majesty. No matter how tall
mountains may rise, they're bound to the *country*
     that raises them and grinds them back into
earth, a borderless *country* to its rooted armies
     of trees standing as sentinel, their branches
country to every leaf, each one a tiny *country*
     to every drop of rain it holds like a breath
for a moment, then must let go. Rain's *country*,
     the sea from which it's exiled into the sky
as vapor. The sky an infinite, universal *country*,
     its citizens the tumultuous stars turning
like a kaleidoscope above my rooftop and me
     tonight. My glass as *country* to the wine I sip,
my lips *country* to my thoughts on the half moon
     —a *country* of light against shadow, like ink
against paper, my hand as *country* to my fingers,
     to my words asking if my home is the only
country I need to have, or if my *country* is the only
     home I have to need. And I write: *country*—
end it with a question mark. Lay my pen to rest.

AMERICAN WANDERSONG

I celebrate myself, and sing myself,
And what I assume you shall assume,
For every atom belonging to me as good belongs to you.
  —WALT WHITMAN,
  Song of Myself

Yo vengo de todas partes,
Y hacia todas partes voy:
Arte soy entre las artes,
En los montes, monte soy.
  —JOSÉ MARTÍ,
  Versos Sencillos

For my parents' exile from their blood-warm rain of Cuba to Madrid's frozen drizzle pinging rooftops the February afternoon I was born. A tiny brown and wrinkled blessing counter to such poverty that my first crib was an open drawer cushioned with towels in an apartment shared by four families. Such as my mother told me for years, kindling my imagination still burning to understand that slipping into being when my longing to belong first began.

And continued: swaddled in the cloud of her arms above the clouds of the Atlantic to America, birthed again at forty-five days old as an immigrant, my newborn photo taken for my green card. Destined to live with two first languages, two countries, two selves, and in the space between them all.

My name is and isn't *Ricardo De Jesús Blanco-Valdés*—christened for the sunlit and sea-song past of my parents' island, carrying withered memories of their homeland like dry rose petals pressed in a book that someday I'd need to crack open, read into the middle of a story I'd need to reclaim, finish, and call my own.

My name is and isn't Richard, a translation I began to call myself by, yearning to write myself into my other story, my other role, my other fictional character as a straight white boy of color in an American drama I didn't quite understand, either.

· · ·

For the terra-cotta roof and tattered lawn chair patio of the home that raised me in Miami, soothed by the mango tree shadows of our backyard. Their tangy-ripe scent stirring in with the incense of *comino* and *laurel* rising from Mamá's pots of *frijoles negros*, the taste of my birthright at dinner every night.

My father listening to 8-tracks of Cuban *danzones,* slumped in the
family room sofa alone with a glass full of rum and empty eyes.
My *abuelo's* front-porch stories of all *we* lost to *la revolución: our*
farmhouse, *our* jasmine trees, *our* dog, Pancho. My *abuela* steadying
me down the driveway, insisting I learn how to ride my bike and be
el hombre she knew I'd never be.

The papery curtains of my bedroom fluttering with the speechless
moon that spoke to me about loneliness, distance, journey, echoed
by the palm tree sways against my window rustling a lullaby every
night while I mumbled my prayers in English, then Spanish: glory be
to all the light and the shadow, the wonder and noise, the confusion
and calm of my childhood—*as it was in the beginning, is now, and
ever shall be, world without end. Amen.*

. . .

For the end of that sinless child when I began to question why god
was love—everywhere and in everything—yet I belonged nowhere
and to no one, unable to love even myself or let myself be loved.
Even after I dared love men instead of women, and my youth burst
like the dusk-red blooms of the poincianas, their beauty surrendered
all at once. I withered like their petals strewn over the same city
streets I wore down driving to nightclubs where I needed to feel at
home under dancefloor lights and against the stubble of men with
phone numbers I knew not to call, inked on cocktail napkins or
my forearm.

Those lovesick nights that dead-ended with a sunrise on the beach,
wading through my ache in every wave dying at my feet. My mind
hovering with the seagulls screeching questions into the wind,
terrified I'd never belong to anything but anonymous sky. The
skyline's trove of ruby and diamond lights waning over the bay
like sinking treasure, my city the fortune I knew someday I'd have
to abandon and lose to memory.

. . .

For the day I had to drive away: nine hundred miles for seventeen
hours straight to New Orleans in my convertible: top down, wind

tousling my hair and mind, my ears breathing in the melancholy notes of any sad song I could find on the radio: *Fire and Rain, Landslide, Dust in the Wind*. Singing along into the windshield, my eyes catching themselves in the rearview mirror, then looking away to keep speeding away from the self I was in Miami toward another self I wanted to bump into striding down Royal Street. Treat him to a swig of bourbon at a jazzy lounge, tell his eyes: *I love you, man, you belong here with me*.

I couldn't find that *me*, until it started raining. There's nothing like rain in New Orleans to forget yourself. It shatters everything. It shattered me like glass, gritty, glittery as the woman's voice that seduced me into La Bon Vie. A hibiscus tucked in her hair and a spotlight on her soul as she finished her set crooning: *good morning, heartache, sit down*. I sat next to her at the end of the bar. Asked her name. She wouldn't say. But I bought her a whiskey anyway for the loss I saw fathomed in her eyes, as brown and dazed as mine. We cheered to lives like the city split by the Mississippi, its waters murky yet always flowing, an incessant filling and emptying of itself, like myself.

. . .

For New York's skyscrapers gleaming like proud kings in a giant game of chess I wanted to master and win. Though I was only a pawn that weekend, riding the click-clack of subways in sync with my heartbeat. Uptown to El Barrio to taste the Spanish of my Puerto Rican kin, their street vendors' icy *piraguas* and steamy *pasteles*. Downtown to stare into the gap left by the towers and my regret for the 9/11 poem I never wrote because I didn't love or hate America enough, then. Then Midtown to gaze at Van Gogh and Matisse, trying to reconcile the truth of art owned by a city whose art is also true greed.

And yet, always the light atop the stairwell beckoning me up toward its grand avenues to imagine a new life as vivid and rude as the yellow streaks of its taxi cabs, as necessary and imposing as its bridges, as sweet-n-sour as the exhaust swirling through its avenues, as charged as its brigade of shoulders hurtling down gum-blotched sidewalks crowded with opportunities fresh as its fruit stands, powerful yet dismal as its jumbotron nights swallowing every star whole. Could I live a life without stars?

. . .

For the blackbirds perched like commas on the telephone wire strung outside my kitchen window like a sentence scrawled in a language as foreign to me as Hartford's granite mansions and grist mills, its white-washed steeples and snuffed-out smokestacks. All like another country to me, feeling my parents' exile as my own, thinking I deserved it for believing that to be an American meant betraying the mango and palm trees that raised me for the winter skeletons of the birches, as beautiful as they were lonely, as I was among them, barely surviving along the gray stretch of Grandview Avenue on my drive to the university to teach how poems sing and save.

Yet what saved me then was my neighbor who fed me cannoli, espresso, and the strums of her guitar recasting steel skies into the cobalt notes of Segovia. What salvaged me was the man who found my eyes over a martini, held my hand down the trail at Talcott Mountain along the reservoir, listened with me to the ice sheets groaning and shifting like my life. The man I married for teaching me how to read William James, how to sauté shallots with filet mignon, how to make my first snow angel amid the frozen souls of the rose garden at Elizabeth Park.

. . .

For all the photos I've taken wandering, wanting to capture myself in-love with a country I could not simply live with, but could also die with. See me here: pocketing a stone from the Colosseum as a souvenir of how an empire or a life crumbles under the weight of its own excess. See me: out of breath atop Fuego volcano wanting to mix my blood with the earth's blood in its crater, simmering with Guatemala's revolutions. See me: inside the dungeon walls of the Palazzo Ducale carved with the last words of the condemned. Hear me: imagining, dreading the last poem I would ever carve.

139

Here I was: sinking with the mortal wealth of Venice's chandeliers and marble floors. Here I was: showered by a Brazilian waterfall in el Rio das Almas, River of Souls, flowing through the hillside resorts of Pirenópolis and the village women beating their wash against its rocks. Here I was: on the top floor of La Grande Arche de la Défense, overlooking the luminous anatomy of Paris, so beautiful it hurt like a lover I can never possess and must abandon. Here I was, wherever I was: lost in always trying to find someplace, someone, something to belong to, yet always returning to myself. Here I am, again.

. . .

For the half of me who never lived in Cuba, yet remembers it as if I was returning to its chartreuse fields and turquoise-laced coasts coloring my eyes again for the first time as the plane descends toward the land of which I am a descendant. I step into a mirage of myself haunted by impossible memories of who I was and would be had my life been lived here.

The boy who hacks into the flesh of coconuts I never tasted, who reads time from the village clock in the square where I never played marbles with my cousins, who pedals through country roads raising dust that never raised me, who catches fireflies that I never chased, the neon green flashes that never dazzled my childhood here.

The son who slashes sugarcane I never harvested with my father, adores him as I never did for his careworn hands that never held mine, my hands around his waist riding his horse that I never rode to the dirt-floor home where I never grew up watching my mother stir pots of *arroz con pollo* in a kitchen where I never ate, and never listened to bedtime stories she never told me in a bed where I never dreamed.

The man who misses a life I never knew was mine to miss, claim as my own in Spanish, as *muy mío*: the conga beats of my tropical storms, ballad of my *palmeras*, balmy whispers of my Caribbean song. *Muy mío*: the iron-red soil of my flesh, sand of my white bones, pink hibiscus of my blood. *Muy mío*: the constellations I reconfigure into an astrology to read the past of who this half of me was, or never was. The future of who I will never be, or who will always be as an island within this island, *muy mío*.

. . .

For the destiny of desire that drove the Potomac's course and mine here, to live along its marshy banks in a colonial townhouse with flower boxes and shelves of poetry I hauled to teach my students questions the other half of me had been asking all my life: What of my love for this country, my faith in its ideals? I heard faint answers through its capital's streets: *We the people* waiting at traffic lights and metro stops. *Justice for all* echoed in statues' eyes and every fountain's trickle. *A more perfect union* breezing through its marble colonnades and beaming off its glorious domes.

Like a tourist wanting to be a native, I said *yes* to all of it. Yes, to the glow of the full moon I caught aglow with promises teetering at the tip of the Washington Monument. Yes, to a fistful of cherry blossoms I praised as delicate as our democracy. Yes, to the veins of my hands pressed against the granite veins of the Vietnam Memorial, standing beside a veteran with only one arm and one rose for one name he thanked for saving his life. Yes, to hating myself for acknowledging the innateness of war, empire, and also the privilege it granted me.

But also—yes—to my duty to contest it, try to shape its story with my deeds and words, with the inaugural poem I'd write ten years later and read before the National Mall looking out into the mirror of a million faces like mine, like so many of us, still hoping to belong and heal as one, under one sun, over one nation. Yes to the half of me I recognized in the reflecting pool capturing the Lincoln Memorial and the wisdom chiseled in his eyes, still speaking to us today: yes, *a house divided cannot stand*. Nor can I.

. . .

For the whole of me steeped in this dusk before the stars embroider the sky and the Milky Way's swatch appears above the back porch of my life in Maine. Needing to be nowhere and no one but this stillness: a drop of rain on my eave just before it swells and adjourns into the ground, a hummingbird paused at my buttercup, my honeysuckle vine before it inches another inch, my still pond just before the ripple from a frog's leap or a loose stone's fall, the content maple leaves before the October wind stirs and chills my hillside and my bones. For now: the fixed geometry of the White Mountains that needn't move or heed a thing, drawn across my window, for now: a spider patient at the center of its web spun across my doorway, for now: my peonies satisfied with the beautiful weight of their immense blooms, for now: my loyal ferns like flags that unfurl, wither, and unfurl again, loyal to the same ground. For now: my wandersong the carol of robins perched in my pear tree, my soul the wisps of these clouds tendering the watercolor sunset. For now: I am citizen of these dimming skies, in the country of my body, homeland to myself—for just a moment.

IMAGINARY EXILE

Dawn breaks my window and dares me
to write a poem brave enough to imagine
the last day I'll ever see this amber light
color the wind breathing life into the dark
faces of these mountains I know by name,
risen from the bedrock of the only country
I've truly lived, resting on the same earth
as this house in which I'll never rise again—

a poem that captures me making my bed
one last time as the sun climbs the maples
I'll never again watch burst like fireworks
into fall, or undress themselves, slip into
snow's white lace. Never again the spring
giggles of my brook, or creaks of my floor.
Never the scent of my peonies or pillows.
Never my eyes on my clouds, or my ears
to the rain on my rooftop in this country—

a poem that finds a word for the emptiness
of suddenly becoming a stranger in my own
kitchen, as I sip my last cup of coffee, linger
with the aroma of my last meal, my hands
trembling as I toss leftovers, wash dishes,
eat one last piece of bread I'll never break
again, and cork a half-empty bottle of wine
I'll never finish, a vintage I'll keep savoring
like memories through my mind's palate—

a poem that lists which parts of me to part
with, or take: Give up my orchids and dog
to my neighbor Jewel, but keep our stares

goodbye. Leave the china and crystal, but
box the plastic souvenirs. Forget my books,
but pack every letter and card I've saved.
Not the gold chains that won't buy back
my life, but stuff all the loose photos like
crumbs in my pockets I'll need to survive—

a poem that brings daisies for my mother,
holds her as I swear I'll return to hold her
again, though we both know I never will.
That speaks with my father one last time
at his grave, and forgives his silence again,
forever. That hopes my husband can flee
with me, knowing he can't—our last gaze
a kiss meaning more to us than our first,
as I hold his hand and hand him my keys—

a poem ending as I walk backwards away
from his love at my door to open another—
step into some strange house and country
to harden into a statue of myself, my eyes
fixed and crumbling like the moon, and like
the moon, live by borrowed light, always but
never quite, dying in the sky, never forgiving
my fate, in a poem I never want to write.

LET'S REMAKE AMERICA GREAT

Yes: Let's re-shoot America as a fantasy, a '50s TV show in clear black and white, sponsored by Kent cigarettes, Wonder Bread, and good old-fashioned war, again. Let's re-create the backlot suburb with rows of five bedroom homes for every Wilson and Johnson, walled by perfectly trimmed hedges, weedless lawns, and at least one 12-cylinder sedan parked in every driveway, in the right neighborhood, again.

Let's recast every woman as a housewife, white and polite as Donna Reed always glowing on the kitchen set, again. Let's direct them to adore making and serving deviled eggs, tuna casserole, apple pies from scratch, again, costumed in pleated skirts and pearl chokers, aprons as immaculate as their thoughts—no lines about a career or rape, again. Let's re-create *Bewitched*, but keep the same script for all women to follow, again: Samantha—blonde and busty, of course—but a real witch who tames her powers for the love of fetching her husband's slippers and stirring his martinis, again.

Let's write-out women like my mother, who fled Cuba broken as her broken English, who cooked dinner in her uniform after twelve-hour shifts at the supermarket, set the table with plastic cups she could rinse out and reuse. Let's cast her as a maid, though even the help needs to be white and proud, again. No roles for Mexican nannies and gardeners unless they are murderers, nor black businessmen unless they are armed drug dealers, nor Muslim taxi drivers unless they are terrorists, again.

Let's give every leading role to men like Jim from *Father Knows Best*, never dangerous, never weak, never poor, always white with a great job and time to page their newspapers, lounge in their wing chairs in command of their wives, their children, and the plot, again. Let's not consider true-to-life parts for men like my immigrant father, who had to work as a butcher all day, help my mother wash the dishes, then clean offices all night. Always too tired to say: *I love you champ*, and kiss me goodnight. Never enough time to be the father, man he wanted to be, again.

Let's audition only straight boys like Opie, who carry slingshots and fishing poles, catch crickets and frogs, who don't play patty-cakes with girls or grow up to marry a man like I did. Let's keep gay characters in the closet for the camera, again: keep Miss Hathaway in skirt suits with cropped hair and single at forty, but keep her mad crush on Jethro, again; keep Uncle Arthur in his floral-print ascots with his hand on his hip, dishing out campy gossip, but keep him acting like a true lady's man, again.

Let's remake America as great as it never really was: Take two. Quiet on the set.

UNTIL WE COULD

for Mark

I knew it then—when we first found our eyes,
in our eyes, and everything around us—even
the din and smoke of the city—disappeared,
leaving us alone as if we were the only two
men in the world, two mirrors face-to-face:
my reflection in yours, yours in mine, infinite.

I knew since I knew you—but we couldn't.

I caught the sunlight pining through the sheers,
traveling millions of dark miles simply to graze
your skin as I did that first dawn I studied you
sleeping beside me: I counted your eyelashes,
read your dreams like butterflies flitting under
your eyelids and ready to flutter into the room.
Yes, I praised you like a majestic creature god
forgot to create, till that morning of you tamed
in my arms, first for me to see, name you mine.
Yes, to the rise and fall of your body, your every
exhale and inhale a breath I breathed as my own
wanting to keep even the air between us as one.

Yes to all of you. Yes I knew, but still we couldn't.

I taught you how to dance salsa by looking
into my Caribbean eyes. You learned to speak
in my tongue, while teaching me how to catch
snowflakes in my palm, love the gray clouds
of your worn-out hometown. Our years began
collecting in glossy photos time-lining our lives
across shelves and walls glancing back at us:

Us embracing in *some* sunset, more captivated
by each other than the sky brushed plum-rose.
Us claiming *some* mountain that didn't matter
as much as our climbing it, together. Us leaning
against columns of ruins as ancient as our love
was new, or leaning into our dreams at a table
flickering candlelight in our full-mooned eyes.

I knew *me* as much as *us*, and yet we couldn't.

Though I forgave your blue eyes turning green
each time you lied, kept believing you, though
we managed to say good morning after muted
nights in the same bed, though every door slam
told me to hold on by letting us go, and saying
you're right became as true as saying *I'm right*,
till there was nothing a long walk couldn't solve:
holding hands and hope under the streetlights
lustering like a string of pearls guiding us home,
or a stroll along the beach with our dog, the sea
washed out by our smiles, our laughter roaring
louder than the waves. Though we understood
our love was the same as our parents', though
we dared to tell them so, and they understood.

Though we knew, we couldn't—no one could.

When fiery kick lines and fires were set for us
by our founding mother-fathers at Stonewall,
we first spoke of *defiance*. When we paraded
glitter, leather, and rainbows, our word then
became *pride* down city streets, demanding:
Just let us be. But that wasn't enough. Parades
became rallies—bold words on signs, shouting
until we all claimed freedom as another word

for marriage and said: *Let us in*, insisted: *love
is love*, proclaimed it into all eyes that would
listen at any door that would open, until *noes*
and *maybes* turned into *yeses*, town by town,
city by city, state by state, understanding us
and all those who dared to say *enough* until
the gavel struck into law what we always knew:

Love is the right to say: *I do* and *I do* and *I do* . . .

and I do want us to see every tulip we've planted
come up spring after spring, a hundred more years
of dinners cooked over a shared glass of wine, and
a thousand more movies in bed. I do until our eyes
become voices speaking without speaking, until
like a cloud meshed into a cloud, there's no more
you, me—our names useless. I do want you to be
the last face I see—your breath my last breath,

I do, I do and will and will for those who still can't

vow it yet, but know love's exact reason as much
as they know how a sail keeps the wind without
breaking, or how roots dig a way into the earth,
or how the stars open their eyes to the night, or
how a vine becomes one with the wall it loves, or
how, when I hold you, you are rain in my hands.

BETWEEN [ANOTHER DOOR]

[the door] Between playing dress-up, parading in his mother's pleated skirt, marvelous as her clip-on ruby earrings, or noosed in his father's necktie, cuffed by his wristwatch ticking with his pulse. [the door] Between playing house with his cousin's Barbie dolls, or careening his toy truck through backyard mud. [the door] Between the coloring book prince he was supposed to be, and made to color in blue, or the princess dress he dreamed of wearing, colored in pink. [the door] Between the Wonder Woman lunchbox he pleaded for at Kmart, or the Superman backpack his grandmother chose for him. [the door] Between his face slapped for putting on a plastic tiara at Craft World, or praised by his grandfather for wielding his plastic sword. [the door] Between cowboys shooting Indians with his brother's cap gun, or sipping make-believe tea with his cat Ferby. [the door] Between what he could grow up to be: a doctor or nurse; a fireman or secretary; an astronaut or housewife; but never both. [the door] Between hula-hooping with the girls at recess, or dodging the boys who'd trip him, shove him, bruise him. [the door] Between the razzle-dazzle of pom-poms he longed to shake, or the boredom of football games he couldn't follow. [the door] Between the soft wrist of the first girl he held hands with, or the stubble of the first man he kissed. [the door] Between mother's head-bowed shame at the dinner table and his fear of father's inch-wide belt on the hook. [the door] Between their small talk about his homework, and their silences about his *friends*. [the door] Between lying to a priest upright in his chair, or lying with his truth on a therapist's couch. [the door] Between playing it straight, or leaving town for the rest of his life. [the door] Between loving the only way he could love, or loving a gun to his head, or opening [another door].

ONE PULSE — ONE POEM

Here, sit at my kitchen table, we need to write this
together. Take a sip of *café con leche*, breathe in
the steam and our courage to face this page, bare
as our pain. Curl your fingers around mine, curled
around my pen, hold it like a talisman in our hands
shaking, eyes swollen. But let's not start with tears,
or the flashing lights, the sirens, nor the faint voice
over the cell phone when you heard "I love you . . ."
for the very last time. No, let's ease our way into this,
let our first lines praise the plenitude of morning,
the sun exhaling light into the clouds. Let's imagine
songbirds flocked at my window, hear them chirping
a blessing in Spanish: *bendición-bendición-bendición.*

Begin the next stanza with a constant wind trembling
every palm tree, yet steadying our minds just enough
to write out: *bullets, bodies, death*—the vocabulary
of violence raging in our minds, but still mute, choked
in our throats. Leave some white space for a moment
of silence, then fill it with lines repeating the rhythms
pulsing through Pulse that night—salsa, deep house,
electro, merengue, and techno heartbeats mixed with
gunshots. Stop the echoes of that merciless music
with a tender simile to honor the blood of our blood,
without writing *blood.* Use warm words to describe
the cold bodies of our husbands, lovers, and wives,
our sisters, brothers, and friends. Draw a metaphor
so we can picture the choir of their invisible spirits
rising with the smoke toward disco lights, imagine
ourselves dancing with them until the very end.

Write one more stanza—now. Set the page ablaze
with the anger in the hollow ache of our bones—
anger for the new hate, same as the old kind of hate
for the wrong skin color, for the accent in a voice,
for the love of those we're not supposed to love.
Anger for the voice of politics armed with lies, fear
that holds democracy at gunpoint. But let's not
end here. Turn the poem, find details for the love
of the lives lost, still alive in photos—spread them
on the table, give us their wish-filled eyes glowing
over birthday candles, their unfinished sandcastles,
their training wheels, Mickey Mouse ears, tiaras.
Show their blemished yearbook faces, silver-teeth
smiles and stiff prom poses, their tasseled caps
and gowns, their first true loves. And then share
their very last selfies. Let's place each memory
like a star, the light of their past reaching us now,
and always, reminding us to keep writing until
we never need to write a poem like this again.

SEVENTEEN FUNERALS

Seventeen suns rising in seventeen bedroom windows. Thirty-four eyes blooming open with the light of one more morning. Seventeen reflections in the bathroom mirror. Seventeen backpacks or briefcases stuffed with textbooks or lesson plans. Seventeen *good mornings* at kitchen breakfasts and seventeen *goodbyes* at front doors.

Seventeen drives through palm-lined streets and miles of crammed highways to Marjory Stoneman Douglas High School at 5901 Pine Island Road. The first bell ringing in one last school day on February fourteenth, 2018. Seventeen echoes of footsteps down hallways for five class periods: algebra, poetry, biology, art, history. Seventeen hands writing on whiteboards or taking notes at their desks until the first gunshot at 2:21 pm.

One AR-15 rifle in the hands of a nineteen-year-old mind turning hate for himself into hate for others, into one hundred fifty bullets fired in six minutes through building number twelve. Seventeen dead carried down hallways they walked, past cases of trophies they won, flyers for clubs they belonged to, lockers they won't open again. Seventeen Valentine's Day dates broken and cards unopened.

Seventeen bodies to identify, dozens of photo albums to page through and remember their lives. Seventeen caskets and burial garments to choose for them. Seventeen funerals to attend in twelve days. Seventeen graves dug and headstones placed—all marked with the same date of death.

Seventeen names: Alyssa. Helena. Scott. Martin—seventeen absentees forever—Nicholas. Aaron. Jamie. Luke—seventeen closets to clear out—Christopher. Cara. Gina. Joaquin—seventeen empty beds—Alaina. Meadow. Alex. Carmen. Peter—seventeen reasons to rebel with the hope these will be the last seventeen to be taken by one of three-hundred-ninety-three-million guns in America.

AMERICA THE BEAUTIFUL, AGAIN

How I sang *O, beautiful* like a psalm at church
with my mother, her Cuban accent scaling up
every vowel: *O, bee-yoo-tee-ful*, yet in perfect
pitch, delicate and tuned to the radiant beams
of stained-glass light. How she taught me to fix
my eyes on the crucifix as we sang our thanks
to our savior for this country that saved us—
our voices hymns as passionate as the organ
piping towards the very heavens. How I sang
for spacious skies closer to those skies while
perched on my father's sun-beat shoulders,
towering above our first Fourth of July parade.
How the timbre through our bodies mingled,
breathing, singing as one with the brass notes
of the marching band playing the only song
he ever learned in English. How I dared sing it
at assembly with my teenage voice cracking
for amber waves of grain that I'd never seen,
nor the *purple mountain majesties*—but could
imagine them in each verse rising from my gut,
every exclamation of praise I belted out until
my throat hurt: *America!* and again *America!*
How I began to read Nietzsche and doubt god,
yet still wished for god to *shed His grace on
thee, and crown thy good with brotherhood.*
How I still want to sing despite all the truth
of our wars and our gunshots ringing louder
than our school bells, our politicians smiling
lies at the mic, the deadlock of our divided
voices shouting over each other instead of
singing together. How I want to sing again—
beautiful or not, just to be harmony—*from
sea to shining sea*—with the only country
I know enough to know how to sing for.

WHAT I KNOW OF COUNTRY

Those picture books from grade-school days:
Pilgrims in tall hats, their gold-buckled shoes
I wanted so badly. White-wigged men standing
tall in velvet-curtained rooms, holding feathers
in their hands, inked words buzzing off the page
into my heart's ear: Life, Liberty, Happiness for
we, the people, singing of shining seas crossed,
the spacious skies of a God-blessed land when
a song and a book were all I knew of country.

I've forgotten the capital of Vermont and Iowa,
but I remember my eyes on a map mesmerized
by faraway cities, towns I couldn't pronounce,
or believe the vast body of this land belonged
to me, and I to it: the Rockies' spine, blue stare
of the Great Lakes, and the endless shoulders
of coastlines, the curvy hips of harbors, rivers
like my palms' lines traced with wonder from
beginning to end, the tiny red dot of my heart
marking where I lived—when what I knew
of country was only what I read from a map.

I wanted to live in the house I dreamed from
television: cushy sofas, crystal candy dishes,
mothers who served perfectly roasted turkeys
with instant stuffing, children with allowances
and perfect teeth, fathers driving teal-blue cars
with silver fins to some country club I'd surely
belong to someday. Though the gunfire, blood
of war beamed into my bedroom, though I fell
asleep, though our men from the moon landed
on my roof with empty promises from space—
fantasy was still all I could believe of country.

I didn't want to change the channel, but I did:
I lifted the shades, let light shine on the carpets
stained with lies I'd missed, and saw the dust
of secrets settled over the photos. The house
began to creak, fall apart around me, alone
for years waiting at the kitchen table, the last
to know, asking my reflection in the windows:
How could you, America? With no answer for
all I knew of country was my hurt and rage.

But home was home: I dusted off the secrets,
cleaned up the lies, nailed the creaky floors
down, set a fire, and sat with history books
I'd never opened, listened to songs I'd never
played, pulled out the old map from a dark
drawer, redrew it with more colors, less lines.
I stoked the fire, burning on until finally: *Okay,
nothing's perfect*, I understood, *I forgive you*,
I said—and forgiveness became my country.

I stayed, you stayed, we stayed for our boys
and girls returning as heroes, some without
legs or arms, for our Challenger and Towers
fainting from the sky, for the terrified lives
of the Big Easy stranded like flightless birds
on roofs, for the sea that drowned our North,
but we swept each grain of sand back to shore,
for the candles we lit for our twenty children
of Sandy Hook, feeling what we've always felt:
to know a country takes all we know of love:

some days better than others, but never easy
to keep our promise every morning of every
year, of every century, and wake up, stumble
downstairs with all our raging hope, sit down
at the kitchen table again, still blurry-eyed,
still tired, and say: *Listen, we need to talk.*

AND SO WE ALL FALL DOWN

after and for Anselm Kiefer's installation
Steigend steigend sinke nieder
(rising, rising, falling down), 2009–2012

And so the hunks of pavement heaved and set
before us are every road we've tired, and those
we wish we had, and those we will, and those
we never will, or those that'll dead-end when
our empire ends. And so let our debris to be
reassembled as tenderly as these curated bits
of rubble letting us see how chaos yields order,
and order chaos. And so let our nation's faces
be these boulders like tiny, bruised moons out
of orbit, and yet enduring, still spinning across
the shiny gallery floor, despite the brutal love
of the universe and brutal love for our country.
And so let us believe we won't simply end like
the speck of a star that will explode as quietly
as a poem whispered above our rooftops into
a black hole into the black night. And so let us
believe there is still eternity even in our ruin,
like this art made out of these remains, made
more alive by destruction. And so all the dead
stalks of these sunflowers embalmed with paint
and fixed by our imagination dangling forever
from the ceiling like acrobats that'll never fall.
And so the hope in what they let us hope: that
our ideals won't all disappear, that some trace
of what we have believed must endure beyond
our decay, beyond entropy's law, assuring us
we'll live on, even after our inevitable dissolve.

DECLARATION OF INTER-DEPENDENCE

Such has been the patient sufferance . . .

We're a mother's bread, instant potatoes, milk at a checkout line. We're her three children pleading for bubble gum and their father. We're the three minutes she steals to page through a tabloid, needing to believe even stars' lives are as joyful and bruised.

Our repeated petitions have been answered only by repeated injury . . .

We're her second job serving an executive absorbed in his *Wall Street Journal* at a sidewalk café shadowed by skyscrapers. We're the shadows of the fortune he won and the family he lost. We're his loss and the lost. We're a father in a coal town who can't mine a life anymore because too much and too little has happened, for too long.

A history of repeated injuries and usurpations . . .

We're the grit of his main street's blacked-out windows and graffitied truths. We're a street in another town lined with royal palms, at home with a Peace Corps couple who collect African art. We're their dinner-party talk of wines, wielded picket signs, and burned draft cards. We're what they know: it's time to do more than read the *New York Times*, buy fair-trade coffee and organic corn.

In every stage of these oppressions we have petitioned for redress . . .

We're the farmer who grew the corn, who plows into his couch as worn as his back by the end of the day. We're his TV set blaring news having everything and nothing to do with the field dust in his eyes or his son nested in the ache of his arms. We're his son. We're a black teenager who drove too fast or too slow, talked too much or too little, moved too quickly, but not quick enough. We're the blast of the bullet leaving the gun. We're the guilt and the grief of the cop who wished he hadn't shot.

We mutually pledge to each other our lives, our fortunes and our sacred honor . . .

We're the dead, we're the living amid the flicker of vigil candlelight. We're in a dim cell with an inmate reading Dostoevsky. We're his crime, his sentence, his amends, we're the mending of ourselves and others. We're a Buddhist serving soup at a shelter alongside a stockbroker. We're each other's shelter and hope: a widow's fifty cents in a collection plate and a golfer's ten-thousand-dollar pledge for a cure.

We hold these truths to be self-evident . . .

We're the cure for hatred caused by despair. We're the good morning of a bus driver who remembers our name, the tattooed man who gives up his seat on the subway. We're every door held open with a smile when we look into each other's eyes the way we behold the moon. We're the moon. We're the promise of one people, one breath declaring to one another: *I see you. I need you. I am you.*

CLOUD ANTHEM

Until we are clouds that tear like bread but
mend like bones. Until we weave each other
like silk sheets shrouding mountains, or bear
gales that shear us. Until we soften our hard
edges, free to become any shape imaginable:
a rose or an angel crafted by the breeze like
papier-mâché or a lion or dragon like marble
chiseled by gusts. Until we scatter ourselves—
pebbles of gray puffs, but then band together
like stringed pearls. Until we learn to listen to
each other, as thunderous as opera or as soft
as a showered lullaby. Until we truly treasure
the sunset, lavish it in mauve, rust, and rose.
Until we have the courage to vanish like sails
into the horizon, or be at peace, anchored still.
Until we move without any measure, as vast
as continents or as petite as islands, floating
in an abyss of virtual blue we belong to. Until
we dance tango with the moon and comfort
the jealous stars, falling. Until we care enough
for the earth to bless it as morning fog. Until
we realize we're muddy as puddles, pristine
as lakes not yet clouds. Until we remember
we're born from rivers and dewdrops. Until
we are at ease to dissolve as wispy showers,
not always needing to clash like godly yells
of thunder. Until we believe lightning roots
are not our right to the ground. Though we
collude into storms that ravage, we can also
sprinkle ourselves like memories. Until we
tame the riot of our tornadoes, settle down
into a soft drizzle, into a daydream. Though

we may curse with hail, we can absolve with
snowflakes. We can die valiant as rainbows,
and hold light in our lucid bodies like blood.
We can decide to move boundlessly, without
creed or desire. Until we are clouds meshed
within clouds sharing a kingdom with no king,
a city with no walls, a country with no name,
a nation without any borders or claim. Until
we abide as one together in one single sky.

New Poems
Part 2

UNCERTAIN-SEA PRINCIPLE

after Werner Heisenberg

the more I try to measure x the less I can measure y

the more I know where I am   the less I know where I'm going
I scribble my name across the sand   *the burnt-orange moon rises, cools, disappears*

the more I know where I'm going   the less I know how to get there
the ebb of each wave seduces me   *silhouettes of sailboats sleep till morning*

the more I know how to get there   the less I know when I'll arrive
freighter lights burn on the horizon   *sea oats sway to the wind's pitch*
like candelabras floating toward port   *like inverted pendulums of timelessness*

the more I know when I'll arrive   the less I know where I am
the tide rises on cue to kiss the shore hello   *seagulls abandon the sea every night*

the less I try to solve for y the more I can solve for x

the less I know where I am   the more I know where I've been
rustling palms protest losing   *the sea gives and gives itself to the shore*
their green to the darkness   *yet returns again and again to itself*

the less I know where I've been   the more I know who I can be
the ocean vanishes into the midnight sky   *the midnight sky vanishes into the ocean*

the less I know who I can be   the more I know who I am
there's no horizon in the stark night   *even in the dark my eyes shape clouds*

the less I know who I am   the more I know that I am, here
I erase my name with a wave of my palm   *I clutch a fistful of sand, breathe, listen*

the more I try to determine my I the less I can determine my *self*

SEASHORE: AN *OVILLEJO*

You: a wave born from everywhere?
From nowhere.

You: destined to crest, spill yourself?
Into myself.

You: who leave no prints on the sand?
Yet I am.

Again I sink back to sea, damned
to keep breaking on foreign shores,
to live always in exile, unsure
from nowhere into myself. Yet I am.

HINENI

———

When the Lord saw that he had turned aside to look, God called to him out of the bush: "Moses! Moses!" He answered, "Here I am."

הִנֵּנִי: וַיֹּאמֶר מֹשֶׁה מֹשֶׁה וַיֹּאמֶר הַסְּנֶה מִתּוֹךְ אֵלָיו וַיִּקְרָא לִרְאוֹת סָר כִּי יְהוָה וַיַּרְא

—EXODUS 3:4

———

God of these waves' gracious hands anointing my feet
—*hineni—here I am*—again trudging
along this shore with the sins of my greed for love,
sins of my gluttony for homeland, sins of my wrath against
myself
—*hineni—here I am*—again asking
the ebb to wash my guilt back into the depths
of forgiveness.

———

God of these salt-laden breaths, these breezes
—*hineni—here I am*—again breathing
their balm into my body of hurt, that I might heal
and exhale words to ease this world's aching.

———

God of these devout seagulls peering into our everyday
eternity, inscribe anew across the pale blue
of the sky's vellum
—*hineni—here I am*—again reading
the clouds' ellipses, following their drift into
glimpses of a divinity I must divine in myself.

God of the infinite possibilities of sand
I was sculpted from

—*hineni*—*here I am*—again infinitely

a boy with bucket and shovel still wanting to sculpt
something almighty out of the sparkly grains of myself,
something sacred that can't be washed away,
something eternal.

God of this sunset's tangerine eye burning holy
between eyelids of sky and sea

—*hineni*—*here I am*—

called by your gaze to ask once again: what would you
have me do with the rest of this
undone life of mine
—here as I am?

WEATHER OF MY WEATHERING

Some days mostly cloudy, a smeared canvas
of vapory questions stalled in the gray skies
of my mind, waiting for answers to blow in
and clear this overcast life. Then days I beam

       mostly sunny with the sweat of boyhood,
       riding my bike. No end to the innocence
       of my gusting endlessly down sidewalks,
       no doubts in my forecast. Other days

mostly rain, the torrent of boys in high school
who spat on me: *faggot, faggot, you faggot*, pelting
my soul. At my feet puddles of hate I'd learn
to jump over. Followed by much calmer days,

       balmy as the poems I recited out loud to
       myself back then, lines breezing through
       my room, across my ears, trusting my life
       to blow where it must sometimes

thunderstorms, rapturous as those nights
ignited with the amber lightning of rum
on my lips pressed against men I'd engulf
with my lust for lust. Some nights clear as

       all the years I spent couched in therapy,
       the eye of my pain's hurricane spiraling
       in me with my mother's regrets, father's
       absence, and grandmother's hate. Today,

though, calls for a warm front as my smile
in the mirror tells me to keep smiling at
all this living, as little as I may know how
to predict the weather of my weathering.

LIFE WITHOUT RAIN

Imagine: the last of the roses—dead
hanging in every kitchen window like
upside-down martyrs, drying humbly,
their spirals of brittle petals on display.

Imagine: the river dry, bare and opened
like the split carcass of some giant beast
exposing its ribs of bleach-white stones
embedded in soft folds of muddy flesh.

Imagine: rainbows of tattered umbrellas,
sugar-yellow raincoats, bottles of rain—
all encased in museum glass, placards
teaching us how succulent earth was.

Imagine: the last perished drops, never
again hear the tin jangle of a hundred
thousand silver pins falling on rooftops
not the gush of waterfalls at doorways.

Imagine: windswept bands never again
strumming windowpanes, vibrating like
a harp, or the incessant drum of drops
on the green and taut palms of leaves.

Imagine: forgetting the jubilant gnats
swarming about the cloud-cooled air,
foretelling the eclipse of an imminent
storm taking custody of the sunlight.

Imagine: remembering your last breath
of the world, wet, full, how you'll miss
your drenched hair, drops dammed at
your eyebrows, spilling down your nose

to bless your lips, how you will never
taste rain again, never catch the tears
of clouds comforting you, those days
they stopped your tears' fall. Imagine.

THANK YOU: FOR NOT LETTING ME DIE

for Michael Kalamaris

For: the mellow moon of your face, breaking
the lonely smoke of that bar with the brilliance
of your simple *hello*. I gave your smile my name,
and you gave my eyes yours, and that was all
the eternity we needed to lean into each other.

For: that first night you took my body, laid me
on the luscious cloud of your satin duvet, made
me holy, an angel, guiltless at last, worthy of all
the blessings of those divine kisses of yours over
my chin and shoulders, at each of my fingertips.

For: those juicy lamb chops I'd never tasted until
you played chef for me the afternoon you spent
aproned, lavishing me with a seven-course dinner
in your one-bedroom apartment, more tantalized
yet by the spun-sugar love we made as dessert.

For: that weekend you gave me New York to lose
ourselves in, believe our love would go on, long as
5th Avenue's glam, delectable as Dean & DeLuca's
macarons, unique as the rings we bought in SoHo,
our vows breezy as that picnic in Central Park.

For: playing Shirley Horn for me through shared
earbuds as we flew back home, listening as one to
her lyrics as if our own: *Isn't it a pity we never, ever
met before.* Lyrics to love the lyrics of us: *Let's forget
the past, let's both agree that I'm for you, you're for me.*

For: those thirty thousand miles in midair and
those three hours you held me in the wings
of your arms, letting the man I had never been
die gladly, letting me be reborn in the promise
of your every breath breathing new life into me.

For: the fountain at *our* park when you told me:
I can't love you this much any longer. Trickles turned
into tears then, but now I hear what you meant:
that your loving would've slowly killed the man
you gave life to. Thank you for not letting him die.

BLUEJAY DIALOGUE:
AN *OVILLEJO*

Say you had wings, where would you go?
Toward my unknown.

Where would you land to stitch your nest?
I can't rest.

If you could choose, where would you die?
As I fly.

Then why sit on your porch and spy
on me? What does your soul hunger
for? To be free as your flutter,
fly toward my unknown till I rest.

THE CUTTING

I saw the blade slip, slit my palm, no longer crying
just because of the onions, but

my blood, as if the blood of another animal
I'd hurt, compelled to save it, save

myself by pressing my wound with my dish towel
to stanch the flow, quiet the guilt

of cutting into my flesh, as if I'd meant to do it.

But then the miracle of witnessing

the gash steadily healing itself, how the will of
my skin cells knew exactly how to mend

such a divide, called each other to meet at that
river of dried blood, and restore

the lifeline across my palm without so much as a scar,
unlike my own thoughts, cutting into me,

bleeding tears, wishing my mind could heal as perfectly.

WRITING HOME

I've straightened the arching fronds of palms
into the stiff lines of poems that pity them for
knowing no other home but the patch of sand
where they were born to die ‖ I've considered
seagulls as a simile that envies their home as
the invisible wind, the expanse of ocean and
earth I can't soar above ‖ I've repeated images
of waves and waves, marveled at how they die,
seep secretly through the pores of sand back
into the homeland of their own seas, again
and again, as I wish I could ‖ I've personified
the moon, needing it to speak in the voice of
my soul to myself, lost in the sky of my own
boundless darkness, yet at ease in the universe
of my loneness ‖ I've given verse to the epic
lifeline of stones: once molten souls spewed
from volcanoes' mouths, then their hardening
their weathering into pebbles I get to behold
in my fists as mute metaphors for my own
journey's questions of where I began, where
I will end ‖ I've jotted down the beats of rain
that rhyme with the soft syllables of snow,
tasking me to ask myself if I could ever be
as fluid and homeless ‖ I've made an allegory
out of wildflower seeds: how they surrender
their destiny to windborne miles that blow
them to root in my tamed garden ‖ Maybe
this is their home more than it will ever be
mine, though I've rendered my poems with
images of them ‖ That's what I'm wondering
tonight: if every line I've written, or will, is
merely a long road that dead-ends ‖ Always
breaking on the thought that my ultimate
home is ultimately some wordless place.

FOR THE HOMELAND OF MY BODY

For my ears:
    still these ears, lullabied by Madrid's rains
    the day I was born into the tempest of
    my parents' exile, holding their lost Cuba
    in their arms along with me.
For my hands:
    still these hands, sculpting sandcastles, guarded
    by the seagulls and palm trees that raised me
    to reach for the sun, to be as confident
    as Miami's skyscrapers rising as I did.
For my feet:
    still these feet wandering forever through
    my father's sugarcane fields, tousled by
    the wind of his dead voice blowing with
    stories of the sweet-sour life his machete
    earned for him, for me.
For my lungs:
    still these lungs, breathing the scent of mangos
    my mother peddled by dirt roads to pay for
    her schoolbooks, the dust in her eyes
    graced by the sea-green Caribbean still
    hemming the island of her life.
For my eyes:
    still these eyes, peering back into the sparkling
    shore I left for the stark brick of New England
    walls enclosing years of my loneliness, quiet
    as the snow-covered fields out my window.
For my hips:
    still these hips, swaying to carnival drums
    with the Brazilian lover whose samba pulsed
    through me, let me lust for the hills and valleys
    of his body, only let it all go.

For my veins:
    still these veins, coursing through me like
    the canals of a sinking city, the cobblestone
    maze of its streets lead me to lose myself
    in the echoes of my own footsteps.
For my legs:
    still these legs, standing at the mouth of
    a volcano, kissing a man I'll fall in love with,
    fiery and gorgeous as the lava at our feet, as
    the sunsets above the home we'll build
    nested in the thick bones of northern pines.
For my flesh:
    still this flesh, alive with all the places I have
    ever loved, or lost, or have yet to find and
    to lose, this constant homeland of my body,
    wherein all my homelands reside at once, as
    they will do, until my body's memory
    disappears into the dust of my own dust.

BECOME ME

for my husband

Become the salt of my blood, my veins'
abating pulse. Become the soft alabaster
of my softening bones, the stale marrow
of this aging life. Become my dull teeth,
and faded lips, still glossing a smile when
you smile into my dimming eyes. Become
my eyes that've studied the anatomy of
our love: my arms in the arc of your arms,
my thighs knotted with yours, our fingers
woven into each other. Become my lungs,
their last gasp, my nerves firing through
every scene of our loving. Become the soil
of my soul. There's nothing more blessed
than taking you with me into the ground.

REVERSE BUCKET LIST

☑ Walked across the dirt of my mother's childhood home in Cuba that she never stepped into again. Felt the bareness of her life under my feet, yet the abundance of the country she gave up, gave me to understand her losses. Saw her never again gazing up at her dreams swaying in her backyard palm trees, never again gossiping about boys' kisses with her sisters at the kitchen table on rainy days, never again cradling her mother's face, even on the day she died without her.

☑ Visited my father's grave one last time. Confessed to the bronze plaque of his full name and color of his eyes that I grew up to incessantly twirl my hair, to sink into my sofa, daydream myself away and master the art of my silence, just as he did. Plucked a fistful of dandelions I laid down and forgave his void in my life. Forgave myself for not knowing how to mourn him, for wanting more from him than he knew how to give.

☑ Swam through the treacherous waters of my grandmother's voice drowning me as a faggot with her hateful words. Survived to hear she spoke a kind of cruel yet loving desire for me to pass as a macho in the world she only knew as cruel, to save me from pain through the pain of her. Learned to adore her as my friend who'd pull a magical mint or quarter out of her pocketbook, who taught me how to roller-skate, how to tell a good joke, how bizarre love can be.

☑ Traveled into my husband's green eyes that welcomed me into the paradise I found in him, in the throbbing hearts of volcanoes we climbed, in the icy-blue silence of glaciers we scaled, in the fury of rivers we rafted, in the solid marble columns and teetering skyscrapers of cities we shared, in the azure shores we strolled, and every tangerine sunset and platinum moonrise we witnessed, that witnessed back the daring light of our adventurous love.

☑ Met my obsessions: waves born to break back into the sea, starlight visible or not, mountains weathering or inching into the sky, clouds lingering or drifting, suns glowing or dying, birds visiting then fleeing, the moon's always changing face, sandcastles meant to last forever, crumbling, the fickle wind combing palm trees, or not. All that's never fixed, never at home, forever fleeting like me. Understood that.

TIME CAPSULE

—a lock of my mother's bouffant the day I gazed at her not as my mother,
but an immortal beauty, even as her hand slipped away from mine and she
tumbled down the stairs, broken, teaching me she wouldn't be forever—

—the whiff of the first raindrops' sizzle on a summer sidewalk the day
my grandmother yelled *go*, and let me go, let me fly for the first time,
pedaling my bike straight into the thunderheads clapping for me—

—the names of crayons I wore down to stubs to recolor the sorrow
of my mother's eyes, *spring green*, my father's frown, *lemon-yellow*, and
my own lonely stick figure as the *razzmatazz* of my imagination—

—the precious seconds of the last dusk I lingered on the porch with
my grandfather in pitch-perfect silence, when I heard the stars speak
light in his eyes saying I needn't be the same kind of man he had to—

—decades-old trinkets from my memories: a whisker from the first man
whose kiss scratched my lips, the rainbow of dance-club lights, the burn
of sunrises waking up in my apartment alone, only my silence beside me—

—those first syllables from my husband's lips when he spoke life into me:
So, do you live here? the timbre of his tender words through all our years
scaling far away volcanoes or stoking the flames of our own fireplace—

—all the mementos of truth I've seen before every mirror understanding
my eyes holding the certitude of *I am*, along with the doubts of *I am not*
the terrible joy of myself as a rose dying in the chipped vase of my body—

—a piece of the moon the night I first saw it as my soul: a thing orbiting
my heart, glowing immortal within me, unlike any trinket I might stuff
in a box and leave behind. So then, bury only my bones, in my end—

—though they'll rot, at least the earth will know the story I had to let go—

LIVING WILL

ARTICLE I

I, RICARDO DE JESÚS BLANCO-VALDÉS, being of sound soul and a resident of the state of my surrender, do hereby revoke all other mortal wills and publish this poem as the last will of my will to live on, testament to all I must leave unfinished.

ARTICLE II

I bequeath, devise, and give to my ashes the ashes of all the following:

A. My mother's HEIRLOOM PEARLS, each bead a hardened memory harvested from the sea of her sorrows for the Cuban homeland she deserted, a strung choker of lustrous losses.

B. My father's GOLD-TONED TIMEX, its wobbly hands, its battered face, much like his own, lost in the hours of this country, until his heart could no longer wind itself. His pulse still ticks at my wrist, but it's time I stop waiting for the father he never became.

C. My grandmother's RECIPE BOX, along with all the words, sweet or pungent, she'd serve me at the dinner table: *my boy / sissy / my dear / faggot / my love.*

D. My grandfather's GILDED CIGAR BOX filled with my childhood's rainbow of colored pencils and memories of the silver-gray smoke signals from his cigar puffs that never quite spelled it out: *I know who you are . . . but I still love you.*

E. My stockpile of PHOTO ALBUMS with posed selves I'll never understand pressed between their pages like dried rose petals: grainy snapshots of sandcastles crumbling with my innocence; overexposed birthday candles lighting my wish to be the someone else I became, but never fully loved; my prom portrait smiling into a future life of children and church I never let go of completely.

F. All the accounts in MY JOURNALS: the scribbles of *I'm sorry* I never voiced to lovers I left without explanation; my inked hopes of *what if's* still banked in my heart for those who left me; the exclamation points the day I met the man I would marry; the ensuing pages of question marks and ellipses of our love's mystery, unresolved.

G. EVERY HOME in which I've tried to find a homeland: the musty apartment in Hartford scented by candles I lit to see me through my darkness; the Guatemalan villa circled by volcanoes as smoldering and unpredictable as my desires; the dusty antiques of the Virginian townhouse that matched my taste for a tangible history, even if not my own.

H. All these INTANGIBLE ASSETS: the investment my eyes have made in silver stars; the gold coins of every sunset I've pocketed; my garden's stock of gerberas and sunflower stalks; the worth of every diamond snowflake and drop of platinum rain I can't take with me.

ARTICLE III

If I could return, I would do so on the CONDITION that I be regranted the entire estate of my memory so that I might cherish what I forgot to cherish; give what I forgot to give; resolve what I forgot to resolve; write the poems I forgot to write; save myself from having to die again INCOMPLETE.

SELF TO SELF

What have you yearned for all your life, Richard? You,
who's aged in me. Do we know enough now to know

that our answer isn't happiness? Not the sweet petals
of some flower we've imagined should forever scent

our heart. Not the nomad clouds we've tried to hold
still in our eyes, long enough to see our soul eternally

at home in them across a homeless sky. Not the face of
the moon, a mime whose gestures of shadow and light

have entertained our desire for immortal glory. Not
the persistence of waves we've wanted to believe are

as fated and willed as we've wished to be. Oh, Richard

.   .   .

have I been asking you the wrong question? Maybe

it's not what we've yearned for, but what we've always
lived on. Isn't our answer the joy of all the temporal

moments that grace us? A bud just before it blooms,
or leans into its wilt. A cloud just before it's sighed

from a wave's wisp and drifts into the destiny of wind.
The dark moon free of our eyes just before it ascends

into the slavery of its sunlit cycles. Tides just before
the purpose of ebb or flow. And Richard, just before

we're Richard, just before the greed of our ego rises,
needing to shine before we slip into yet another day.

ANTI-POEM

Coffee, strong and bitter as the street
outside, waking up to rainfall wetting
city lights and leaves. People suddenly
afraid of water, moving shelled inside
their umbrellas, colorful props in some
bizarre choreography of headless bodies.
For once, I'm not compelled to imagine
their faces above their arms clutching
briefcases, toting purses, and jeweled
with watches, diamond bracelets. Not
tempted to give them or myself a name,
nor stories of sorrow or joy, nor places
we run to become who we're not. None
of it matters to me today. I'm transparent
behind the storefront window, watching
the city move with eyes that aren't mine,
but someone's who for a moment rests
with wanting nothing but what rain gives.

A GOOD DAY TO DIE

When there's nothing but a knowing, when
you wake up to the stare of your dog's eyes
like tiny brown suns shining with the truth
of all you are before the alarm rings, when

you lock your door, turn up the volume and
dance barefoot, swaying alone with your eyes
closed, your robe open to the world and all
you lust for is a song to hold your body, when

you beam a *Good morning* at the post office,
or *Great to see you* at the market, meaning
every word, cut by your lips into little jewels
that sparkle with syllables of kindness, when

you toss your to-do list in the garbage, waste
yourself in the lazy beauty of being witness
to the gestures of an oak, a squirrel's dramatic
pause, to the frenzy at the bird feeder, when

you sit under the clouds for dinner, filled with
gratitude for more than bread, and say grace
for dusk's feast of savory hues and the dessert
of sugary stars that indulge your soul, when

you smile back at your smile floating in the fog
of the bathroom mirror, your faint yet fulfilled
eyes return the gaze of god within you pleased
with the honest life you've given yourself, when

all that's left is a knowing that you don't need
to know yet another home in some new city for
the love of something other than you, blanketed
in the peace of your worn bed, ready to die with

all you are or aren't, all you've given or gotten,
all you've believed or doubted, all you've done
or haven't done, ready to kiss the moon's cheek
goodbye, forever, but the moon says: *No, not yet.*

MOONRISE

I write: a giant tiger's eye peering out
from the dome of a dark thicket, then
I write: the worn face of a doubloon,
a gold fortune lighting the poor night,
and the moon says: *I am simply the moon.*
Yet I write on—an amber pearl rising,
fading into a geisha's porcelain pallor,
a humble seductress, a chaste coquette.
I write of the color of white chocolate,
the fine texture of talc like the cinders
of light settling out of the darkness onto
my thought-filled page of inked words,
when the moon pauses, tells me: *Listen, I am
as rough as you, merely hard rock, gray dust.*

SAY THIS ISN'T THE END

Say we live on, say we'll forget the masks
that kept us from dying from, the invisible,
but say we won't ever forget the invisible
masks we realized we had been wearing
most our lives, disguising ourselves from
each other. Say we won't veil ourselves again,
that our souls will keep breathing timelessly,
that we won't return to clocking our lives
with lists and appointments. Say we'll keep
our days errant as sun showers, impulsive
as a star's falling. Say this isn't our end.

Say I'll get to be thrilled as a boy spinning
again in the barber's chair, tell him how
I'd missed his winged scissors chirping
away my shaggy hair eclipsing my eyes,
his warm clouds of foam, the sharp love
of his razor's tender strokes on my beard.
Say I'll get more chances to say more than
thanks Shirley at the checkout line, praise
her turquoise jewelry, her son in photos
taped to her register, dare to ask about
her throat cancer. Say this isn't her end.

Say my mother's wrinkled eyes won't die
from the goodbye kiss I last gave her, say
that wasn't our final goodbye, nor will we
be stranded behind a quarantine window
trying to see our refracted faces beyond
the glare, read our lips, press the warmth
of our palms to the cold glass. Say I won't
be kept from her bedside to listen to her

last words, that we'll have years to speak
of the decades of our unspoken love that
separated us. Say this isn't how we'll end.

Say all the restaurant chairs will get back
on their feet, that we'll all sit for another
lifetime of savoring all we had never fully
savored: the server as poet reciting flavors
not on the menu, the candlelight flicker
as appetizer, friends' spicy gossip and rich
saucy laughter, sharing entrées of memories
no longer six feet apart, our beloved's lips
as velvety as the wine, the dessert served
sweet in their eyes. Say this is no one's end.

Say my husband and I will keep on honing
our home cooking together, find new recipes
for love in the kitchen: our kisses and tears
while dicing onions, eggs cracking in tune
to Aretha's croon, dancing as we heat up
the oven. Say we'll never stop feasting on
the taste of our stories, sweet or spicy, say
our table will never be set for just one,
say neither of us dies, many more toasts
to our good health. Say we will never end.

Say we'll all still take the time we once
needed to walk alone and gently through
our neighborhoods, keep noticing beauty
in ant hills and sidewalk cracks blossoming
weeds, of yappy dogs and silent swing sets
rusting in backyards, of neat hedges hiding
mansions and scruffy lawns of boarded-up
homes. Say we won't forget our seeing
that every kind of life is a life worth living,
worth saving. Say this is nobody's end.

Or say this *will* be my end, say the loving
hands of gloved, gowned angels risking
their lives to save mine won't be able to
keep me here. Say this is the last breath
of my last poem, will of my last thoughts:
I've witnessed massive swarms of fireflies
grace my garden like never before, drawn
to the air cleansed of our incessant greed,
their glow a flashback to the time before
us, omen of earth without us, a reminder
we're never immune to nature. I say this
might be the end we've always needed
to begin again. I say this may be the end to
let us hope to heal, to reach the stars. Again
I'll say: heal, reach, and become the stars
that became us, whether this is our end—
or not.

NOTES

Questioning Villa Vizcaya Museum and Gardens. The Vizcaya
  Museum and Gardens (previously known as simply Villa
  Vizcaya) make up the former estate of businessman James
  Deering, built between 1914 and 1922 in Coconut Grove, a
  present-day neighborhood of Miami, Florida.
Radiant Beings: Photos by Joyce Tenneson. Inspired by Joyce
  Tenneson's photography book, *Radiant Beings: The Magical
  Essence of Flowers.*
—anatomy of light— was commissioned by LnS Gallery for *Tran-
  scendentalism, Distilled,* a solo exhibition of artist Rafael Sori-
  ano, one of the major Latin American artists of his generation
  and one of the premier painters of Cuba.
To the Artist of the Invisible. A commissioned poem commemorat-
  ing the 2013 Fragrance Foundation Awards and performed at
  Lincoln Center in New York City, April 2013.
Big Wood River. Written while the writer in residence at the
  Hemingway House and Preserve in Ketchum, Idaho, where
  he died by suicide. The house sits on twelve acres along the
  Big Wood River and is managed by the Community Library.
  The writer-in-residence program encourages ongoing creative
  work and deep thinking in a landscape that Hemingway loved.
  I remain ever so grateful to the Community Library for the
  experience of a lifetime and the poem that arose from it.
What You Didn't Let Us Lose. Andrew John Sweet was an Ameri-
  can photographer known for his documentary photography of
  the residents of South Beach in the 1960's and 1970's, with a

particular focus on the Jewish community, many of them Holocaust survivors. Sweet was murdered in 1982, when he was twenty-eight years old.

Visiting Elizabeth. A variation of a *glosa,* a Spanish form that quotes four lines of poetry as an epigraph from another poem or poet. These four lines act as a refrain in the final line of the four stanzas written by the poet. So the first line of the epigraph would be the final line of the first stanza, the second line ends the second stanza, etc.

What Governs Us: Written for the occasion of Governor Janet Mills's second-term inauguration on January 4, 2023. She is the first female governor of Maine.

Décima Guajira. A variation of a *décima,* a traditional form popular in Latin America and Spain. It's octosyllabic with ten lines to the stanza. Often recited, or sung, with improvisation and written with variations in different countries. https://en.wikipedia.org/wiki/D%C3%A9cima#Poetry

Como Tú / Like You / Like Me is dedicated to the young people impacted by DACA and the DREAM Act, who are often called DREAMers. DACA refers to Deferred Action for Childhood Arrivals, an American immigration policy that allows some individuals who were brought to the United States illegally as children to receive a renewable two-year period of deferred action from deportation. The DREAM Act (short for the Development, Relief, and Education for Alien Minors Act) was a bill in Congress that would have granted legal status to certain undocumented immigrants who were brought to the United States as children and went to school here. Although several versions of the bill have been introduced in Congress since 2001, it has never passed.

Island Body was commissioned by Bacardi Limited and served as the script for a short film and radio segment. While this was a more commercial commission, as a Cuban American I obviously felt personally drawn to the plight of exiles like the Arechabala family (originators of Havana Club rum), who were forced to flee Cuba at gunpoint. The poem has been slightly revised for this volume.

Until We Could was commissioned to commemorate and celebrate the tenth anniversary of Freedom to Marry, the organization that developed the leading national strategy for marriage equality in the US. The poem is dedicated to Mark Neveu and our journey together for over twenty years. A short film of the poem was produced by Peter Spears and narrated by Ben Forster and Robin Wright. The poem has been slightly revised for this volume.

One Pulse—One Poem was written in response to the Pulse nightclub shooting of June 12, 2016. The tragedy particularly disturbed and affected me as a gay man, who understands that places like Pulse are not merely nightclubs; they are community; they are a surrogate home for many like me. To have such a home desecrated in such a manner was doubly devastating. In that respect, I intended for the poem to speak of the very act of writing a poem as a way to process our shared grief and honor the lives of the victims and survivors. The poem appeared in *Bullets into Bells: Poets & Citizens Respond to Gun Violence*, a powerful anthology that brings together the voices of poets and citizens most impacted to call for the end of gun violence with the activist power of poetry. *One Pulse—One Poem* was first published in the *Miami Herald*.

And So We All Fall Down is a quasi-ekphrastic poem reflecting on Anselm Kiefer's *Steigend steigend sinke nieder (rising, rising, falling down)* 2009–2012 large-scale installation, an assembly of debris collected from the demolition of the Rue des Archives in Paris.

Uncertain-Sea Principle was inspired by the uncertainty principle formulated by German physicist and Nobel laureate Werner Heisenberg in 1927. It states that we cannot know both the position and speed of a particle, such as a photon or an electron, with perfect accuracy; the more we know of a particle's position, the less we know about its speed, and vice versa. I "applied" this principle to my search for home in this stereoscope, also known as a contrapuntal poem, which can be read in more than one way, such as left to right across the two columns or down first one column and then the other.

Seashore and *Bluejay Dialogue*. An *ovillejo* is an old Spanish form popularized by Miguel de Cervantes. A ten-line poem comprised of three rhyming couplets (or two-line stanzas) and a quatrain (or four-line stanza). The first line of each couplet is eight syllables long and presents a question to which the second line responds in three to four syllables—either as an answer or an echo. The quatrain is also referred to as a redondilla with an *abba* rhyme pattern. The final line of the quatrain combines lines 2, 4, and 6 together.

Hineni. The word *hineni* is found in the Hebrew Scriptures and means "here I am". [. . .] On spelling alone, the word would seem to appear 178 times in the scriptures. Once vowels are applied, however, it is easy to confuse *hineni* with the ubiquitous *hi'nih'ni*, which means "I am here." These two words apparently mean the same thing, but they do not. [. . .] *Hineni* accomplishes two things: the caller has the full attention of the protagonist whose story will change in a dramatic way. The reader must wait to find out what the protagonist will be asked to do. [. . .] *Hineni* is different. It says, "I am here to listen to whatever the caller has to say, but [. . .] I do not yet know what the caller wants from me." http://www.jewishchronicle.org/2014/11/30 /hineni-here-i-am-and-i-am-here-are-different/

Thank You: For Not Letting Me Die. The lines: "Isn't it a pity we never, ever / met before" and "Let's forget / the past, let's both agree that I'm for you, you're for me" are from Shirly Horn's rendition of *Isn't It a Pity*, composed by George Gershwin, lyrics by Ira Gershwin.

CREDITS

ACKNOWLEDGMENTS

I am grateful to the editors of the publications in which the following new poems first appeared: *Scientific American* ("Uncertain-Sea Principle"); *The Atlantic* ("Why I Needed To" and "Say This Isn't the End"); Academy of American Poets, *Poem-A-Day* ("Maine Yet Miami"); *The Map of Every Lilac Leaf*, Smith College Museum of Art ("Music in Our Hands"); *Grist: Journal of the Literary Arts* ("Big Wood River"); and *The Red Letters Project* ("The Splintering"). The poems "Complaint of El Río Grande," "between [another door]," and "Cloud Anthem" first appeared in *Boundaries*, a limited-edition fine press book published by Two Ponds Press.

. . .

My most heartful gratitude for Sandra Cisneros, whose work and life example first gave me permission to tell my story; for Professor Campbell McGrath, whose mentorship first fostered my voice; for Rob McQuilkin, the best agent and literary buddy I could've ever wished for; for Helene Atwan from Beacon Press, who embraced my work and champions all the good that poetry can do in the world; and for the great minds, generous hearts, and beautiful souls of those who continue to nurture my voice and my life: Sonia Bonilla, Nikki Moustaki, Brian Leung, Ruth Behar, Caridad Moro-Gronlier, Emma Trelles, Spencer Reece, Kim Dower, Eduardo Aparicio, Jan Beatty, Ed Ochester, Alison Granucci, Francisco Aragón, Ada Limón, Natasha Trethewey, and Patricia Smith.

ABOUT THE AUTHOR

Selected by President Obama as the fifth inaugural poet in US history, Richard Blanco was the first Latinx, immigrant, and gay person to serve in that role. In 2023, Blanco was awarded the National Humanities Medal by President Biden. Blanco was a Woodrow Wilson Fellow and has received numerous honorary doctorates. He has taught at Georgetown University, American University, and Wesleyan University, and currently is an associate professor at Florida International University.

Born in Madrid to Cuban exile parents and raised in Miami in a lower-working-class family, Richard Blanco has navigated cultural identity, sexuality, and sociopolitical matters in his five collections of poetry: *How to Love a Country* (Beacon Press, 2019); *Looking for The Gulf Motel*, winner of the Paterson Poetry Prize and the Thom Gunn Award (University of Pittsburgh Press, 2012); *Directions to The Beach of the Dead*, recipient of the Beyond Margins Award from the PEN American Center (University of Arizona Press, 2005); *City of a Hundred Fires* (University of Pittsburgh Press, 1998); and now *Homeland of My Body* (Beacon Press, 2023).

Blanco is also the author of the memoirs *For All of Us, One Today: An Inaugural Poet's Journey* (Beacon Press, 2013) and *The Prince of Los Cocuyos: A Miami Childhood* (Ecco, 2014), winner of a Lambda Literary Award and a Maine Literary Award. Exploring other genres, with Vanessa Garcia, Blanco cowrote the play *Sweet Goats & Blueberry Señoritas*, which premièred at Portland Stage and is currently slated for a second production at Actors' Playhouse in Miami. His inaugural poem "One Today" was published as a children's book, in collaboration with renowned illustrator Dav Pilkey (Little, Brown 2015), and *Boundaries* (Two Ponds Press 2017), a collaboration with photographer Jacob Hessler, is a book that challenges the physical and psychological dividing lines that shadow the United States. He is currently a writing co-executive producer for a TV series adapted from his memoir and is also co-lyrist for *Waiting for Snow in Havana*, a musical in development.

As a civically engaged author, Blanco has written occasional poems for organizations and events including the reopening of the US Embassy in Cuba, Freedom to Marry, and the Boston Strong benefit concert following the Boston Marathon bombings. Nationally as well as internationally, Blanco lends his art and voice to advocate for diversity, LGBTQ rights, immigration rights, and arts education.